EXPECT A MIRACLE!

The book to change your life.

DR. JOHN HINWOOD
And Friends

**Executive
Books**

You Can…Expect a Miracle!

Dr. John Hinwood
website: www.expect-a-miracle.net

Published by
Executive Books
206 West Allen Street
Mechanicsburg, PA 17055
717-766-9499 800-233-2665
Fax: 717-766-6565
www.ExecutiveBooks.com

ISBN: 978-1-933715-78-0

Cover Design by Liga Byron and Winston Marsh

Printed in the United States of America

Table of Contents

This book is dedicated to…

- people who think miracles are for someone else

- people who wish and wish, and don't really believe in their own worthiness, or that such great energies are available for us all to receive

- people who are 'on the lookout' every day for miracles

- people who have already experienced miracles in their lives, and are ready to receive more.

Acknowledgments

Thank you to my beautiful wife Judy for her help, patience, inspiration, encouragement and love. She has proofread every story, written some stories herself and been my 'rock' throughout this project.

Thank you to all those friends and colleagues who have continually encouraged me to listen to my innate being, put pen to paper and write this book that will be inspirational for so many people.

Thank you to D.C. Cordova, who first introduced me to "Expect a Miracle" cards in 1987, and to the Unity Church where D.C. bought her first pack of cards.

Thank you to my great friend and mentor Charles "Tremendous" Jones, whom I first met in Pittsburgh at a Living Principles Seminar in 1978. Charlie has continually encouraged me to write about my experiences from handling out thousands of "Expect a Miracle" cards all over the world.

Thank you to all the contributors of such wonderful miracle stories: Jennifer Carter, John Demartini, Gayle Gibbon, Craig Gilberd, Doug Herron, Pat Hicks, Judy Hinwood, Berni Ireland, Kenneth-Clyde Ivory, Ely Lazar, Gilles Lamarche, Keith Livingstone, Allan Lowe, Fabrizio Mancini, Clinton McCauley, Scott Schilling, Joan Smith, Roy Smith, Mario Stefano and Brenda Veenbaas. They come from many and varied backgrounds from countries all over the world, and their stories portray events that have occurred over many years.

Thank you to my personal assistants, Leanne Horn and Leah Cranston, who have typed, edited, retyped and made

9

Acknowledgments

suggestions during the preparation of the manuscript. Thanks also to my sister-in-law Carlie Armitage, who edited all the initial stories.

Thank you to my editor, Geoff Whyte, for his creative inspirations, understanding and input into the preparation of this book.

Thank you to my webmaster Michael O'Shea and his wife Rachael, who have done so much background work for the book. Michael developed the companion website www.expect-a-miracle.net which launched in late November 2007. He was also the inspiration for the cover design.

Thank you to the entire team at Executive Books for their commitment to excellence in publishing this book.

Thank you to my great friend, Winston Marsh, Australia's 'Marketing Guru' and his graphic designer Liga Byron for their inspirational thoughts for the front and back cover designs and for Winston's creative genius in naming many of the stories.

I would rather work with five people who really believe in what they are doing than 500 who can't see the point.

Patrick Dixon

Foreword

Two of the greatest words in our vocabulary, "expect" and "miracle" – "expect a miracle." The power of expectation is the awakening of hope, desire, enthusiasm, excitement, dreams, all the qualities that make life fulfilling. Your level of expectation is where it all begins. Talent or ability can't stop you, your financial condition can't stop you, your education can't, your age or marital status, or the color of your skin can't stop you. It all begins with your level of expectation. Simply put, if we can raise our level of expectation, we can expand and increase our miracles. Our level of expectation sets the limits for our life. If we only expect a little, that's what we'll get. We can change the world by changing our level of expectation.

To many, expecting a miracle would seem to be expecting too much, but when you look up, look around, and look into your heart, you begin to see the wonder of life. Everything is a miracle – you are a miracle, the universe is a miracle, and so if we are surrounded by miracles everywhere we look, what's so unusual about expecting your own miracle? My own life has been filled with more than eighty years of miracles, and I expect them to keep coming.

One of the greatest examples of a life of miracles was that of Dr. Norman Vincent Peale. His life of positive thinking was the foundation for the miracles in his life. Dr. Peale lived ninety-five miracle-filled years before graduating while asleep one Christmas Eve. Dr. Peale was a miracle role model for millions around the world because his role model was the greatest miracle worker the world has ever known, Jesus Christ.

Foreword

In his little booklet, *Thought Conditioners*, Dr. Peale said, "Over the years, I had noticed that certain passages from the scriptures had a particularly potent effect on human beings. I began, therefore, to list the life-creating words from the scriptures that had done me the most good. Many of these I had recommended to others. Some of them have been called to my attention by people in whom there had occurred the most astonishing demonstration of new life and joy. When I applied them to myself, I found they did indeed possess tremendous effectiveness."

Here are a few of my thought conditioners to help you expect your miracles:

The things which are impossible with men are possible with God. Luke 18:27

Renew a right spirit within me. Psalm 51:10

What things soever ye desire, when ye pray, believe that ye receive them, and ye shall have them. Mark 11:24

Be ye transformed by the renewing of your mind. Romans 12:2

Eye hath not seen, nor ear heard, neither have entered into the heart of men, the things which God hath prepared for them that love him. 1st Corinthians 2:9

Remember to give thanks; be thankful at all times, because if you are not thankful for the miracles of the past, you won't be thankful for the miracles to come.

Dr. Hinwood's life is filled with miracles because of his great and growing level of expectation. His life of miracles has blessed the lives of thousands around the world, because he never sought miracles for selfish reasons. His miracles enabled him to share, serve and give more. And now, he is doing it in this book. His "Expect a Miracle" dream is for you to live a life filled with miracles to inspire others to expect the same.

Tremendously,
Charles "Tremendous" Jones

> *A single act of kindness throws out roots in all directions, and the roots spring up and make new trees.*
> *The greatest work that kindness does to others is that it makes them kind themselves.*
>
> *Amelia Earhart*

Introduction

After 20 years of handing out over 50,000 "Expect a Miracle" cards to clients and people I've met all over the world, and witnessing some huge, positive transformations in many people, I'm now taking this simple, yet very powerful tool further via Volume 1 of this series of books, "You Can...Expect a Miracle!" and the associated website, www.expect-a-miracle.net.

Probably the best thing for me personally is that so many people I give a card to, no matter what their station in life, turn the card over to find that it is blank on the back. After a pause, I say, "Would you like a miracle?" They almost always say, "Oh yes!"

The change in state of most individuals on receiving the card, reading the words, "Expect a Miracle," and then turning the card over to find no name, no advertising, no gimmick, purely a message of hope, is amazing to witness.

Most people move to an enlivened state of wellbeing. For some, who only show a glimmer of hope that it's possible for their life to be even a bit better than it is right now, it can be a hugely uplifting event. As my wife Dr. Judy Hinwood says, "let's at least be seed-sowers." Judy says that "Miracles are the flowing of spirit from virtual reality into the five physical senses reality in which our bodies live."

James Allen said in his book *As a Man Thinketh*, "What the mind of man can see and believe, it can achieve." A shift in a person's focus from where they are currently to where they would like to be can be a truly momentous event in that person's life.

Introduction

Tony Robbins says we can change our emotional state and therefore our destiny "in a heartbeat," and I believe this is a truth. One's expectation can change from doom and gloom to a miracle state in the time it takes to register a new thought.

Where did the idea of an "Expect a Miracle" card come from? I first saw a sign saying "Expect a Miracle" in the share supply store at a Parker Chiropractic Seminar we attended in Dallas, Texas in 1977. I loved the concept that if my patients "Expected a Miracle" every time they came to my office, this thought would manifest into a wellness mode of thinking rather than a disease- and sickness-focused state of mind.

In 1987, Judy and I attended a seminar in Melbourne, Australia called Money and You, presented by the Excellerated Learning Institute. The facilitator was Robert Kiyosaki, and the director of logistics was a Chilean woman named D.C. Cordova.

At one point, D.C. Cordova gave me a card that said…

Expect A Miracle

I was so taken by the card that I asked D.C. if I could reproduce it and hand it out to others. "Go ahead, I originally found the cards in a Unity Church bookshop," she replied. And so I did.

Introduction

I believe we have all had miracle experiences at some time in our lives, and I ask that you take the time to post at least one story on the website to enrich the lives of others. From small beginnings... As well as creating a positive energy focus at www.expect-a-miracle.net, the "Expect a Miracle" community will generate a collection of inspiring stories that will be shared with a worldwide community. Compounding, compounding, compounding...spreading words of positive, healing energy, the growth potential is enormous.

I welcome you to join me in this project. Your story or stories may give others a new lease on life. The world continually needs a good dose of positivity. As Zig Ziglar says, we all need "a checkup from the neck up to remove stinkin' thinkin'!"

Dr. John Hinwood

> *There are only two ways to live your life...one is as though nothing is a miracle, the other is as though everything is a miracle.*
>
> *Albert Einstein*

1

MIRACLES OF ATTITUDE

Then, without realizing it, you try to improve yourself at the start of each new day; of course, you achieve quite a lot in the course of time. Anyone can do this, it costs nothing and is certainly very helpful. Whoever doesn't know it must learn and find by experience that a quiet conscience makes one strong.

Anne Frank

Your Table is Waiting

A number of years ago, I was working with John and Judy Hinwood on a massive Internet-based project. The project required meticulous preparation, and the fact that we lived in different states meant that hugely busy working weekends, in either their home state or mine, were required in order to get the project up and running.

On one occasion, we'd met at a large inner-city Melbourne hotel, and pretty soon John's room became a hive of activity as we brainstormed, checking and re-checking all of our scripts, headlines, and schematic flows. After hours of intense focus, with the summer evening darkening outside, we suddenly realized that we'd forgotten to have lunch, and dinner, and were absolutely famished! (This happens quite a bit when one is working with the amazing Dr Hinwood.) "Keith, I'm starving!" said John. "Do you know a good place to eat? With seafood? I want something really nice, because we've been going hard!"

"John, I know just the place, but it's after 9 p.m. on a Saturday night, so it's going to be absolutely packed!"

"Keith, expect a miracle! There's a lovely table and a beautiful meal just waiting for us!"

We made our way to Toto's Pizza House, one of Melbourne's celebrated eateries on the "Restaurant Mile" of Lygon Street. Toto's is a famous landmark in Melbourne, renowned for its great, inexpensive food, prompt and courteous service, and delicious pizzas, even the crusts of which get completely eaten! As I'd expected, the place was packed! John's expectations were different, however, and he'd dressed immaculately, in anticipation of a marvellous meal.

He marched up to the head waiter and acknowledged him with a pleasant nod. The waiter was a distinguished-looking older man, impeccably attired. He acknowledged us in return.

"I believe I have a table waiting," said John.

"Your name, sir?" said the waiter.

"Hinwood. Dr. John Hinwood," said John.

The waiter scanned his list of patrons, and was perturbed to find that Dr. Hinwood wasn't on the list. "I'm sorry, Dr. Hinwood. We don't appear to have you on our list. When did you make your booking?"

"I didn't. My good friend here, Dr. Livingstone, told me that this was the best place in Melbourne for a wonderful meal, and so we decided to come straight down. However, I'm sure we have a table here, sir."

At this point, John whipped out one of his ever-present "Expect a Miracle" cards. Now John is one of those people who isn't easily refused. He's a 'validator,' someone who draws people right in and builds them up. He will often 'validate' people he's only just met with a huge hug and kiss, and the more they resist, the bigger the kiss and hug they get. John will validate either gender of any species in this way – he really doesn't care. It's a life-long habit.

The waiter took the card, scrutinized it carefully, and then broke into a big grin, before saying, "Excuse me for a second, Dr. Hinwood. I'll be right back." He headed out back, then emerged a few moments later with an affirmative nod of his head. "Come right this way, Dr. Hinwood. We certainly do have a table for you!"

We were shown to a great table in a corner of the restaurant, and were seated and brought large linen napkins and glasses of cold, fresh water. A few seconds later, several very cheerful, distinguished-looking Italian men emerged from the back room, all discussing the "Expect a Miracle" card.

"We've never seen one of these cards before," said the head waiter, "and these gentlemen were wondering where they can get some!"

"Right here!" said John, and he whipped out about 50 cards for the gentlemen, and several interested diners nearby. The meal was wonderful, of course. We were treated like kings, and returned to our work fully refreshed and replete, just as we had expected.

Dr. Keith Livingstone

The greatest pleasure in life is doing what people say you cannot do.

Walter Bagshot

The Shopkeeper

A long time ago, a shopkeeper received a package of merchandise from England. He always admired the efficient way the British packed things, as it was always done with meticulous care.

When he opened the package, there was a card on top which said, "Expect a Miracle." "What does that mean? How did that get there?" he wondered, and almost threw it in the trash, but stuffed it into his shirt pocket instead. That night, when he emptied his pockets, he found the card and showed it to his wife. "Look at this. 'Expect a Miracle.' What is that supposed to mean?"

"Maybe that's what we need," she said. "Our problems seem so overwhelming. I wonder what would happen if we started expecting great things, instead of always expecting the worst? Could miracles take place?"

They decided to try it for a few days, starting with small problems. "Maybe we will get some new ideas," said the shopkeeper. "Maybe there is a solution. Anyway, what do you say? Let's expect a miracle, really expect it for a few days, and see what happens."

Then something changed for them. They began believing that not only could their problems be solved, but that they *would* be solved and more importantly, the solution was, even then, being worked out. Miracles, little miracles, started happening. Strange coincidences began developing. All kinds of experiences began coming their way, one after another. They became different, hopeful, optimistic. The little problems began giving way, and the big ones became less formidable.

When anyone starts expecting a miracle, they become so conditioned that they begin to actually make miracles happen. They get on the miracle wavelength. Abilities become positively focused, rather than negatively focused. Creative forces are released in the mind. The flow-away tendency is reversed, and life now flows toward them. The negative expectations that drove away the good are replaced by positive expectations.

With a clear goal that is a sharply focused objective and embraces good, not only for you but for all of those around you, what you want to do, what you want to be and where you want to go, one activates the law of successful achievement.

The law of attraction is activated positively, and instead of sending out negative thoughts and activating the world around us negatively, the positive thinker with clear goals for good will activate the world around him positively.

He works and keeps on working. He thinks and keeps on thinking. He believes and keeps on believing. He never lets up, never gives in. He gives the effort the full treatment of positive faith and action. The result? He can, because he thinks he can. His dreams come true…he attains his goals…miracles happen.

Miracles come in all sizes: big ones, medium-sized ones, and small ones. Start believing in small ones, and work your way up to big ones. Think, believe, work, treat people right and give it all you've got, and you will find yourself doing the most amazingly constructive things in this life.

Pat Hicks

The Fickle Finger of Fate

An unfortunate accident in 1972, when I was living and teaching in South Africa, resulted in the amputation of my entire left index finger after I misjudged the power of a circular saw in the school woodwork shop.

The surgeon who performed the amputation did a stunning job in connecting the muscles of my index finger to my middle finger, and some people who have known me for more than twenty years still don't realize that I only have four digits on my left hand. Since the loss of my finger, many funny incidents have occurred, for example little kids like to count the fingers on both of my hands, and then set about looking for the lost finger.

My wife Judy and I often travel to North America to speak at chiropractic conferences. On one of our trips a couple of years ago, the United States Immigration Department had just introduced a new procedure of photographing and fingerprinting the right and left index fingers of all 'aliens' entering the country. We arrived at Los Angeles International Airport, or LAX as it is known by the locals, and had to pass through the mighty immigration hall of the Bradley building. This is an impressive structure with a very high roof, flags hanging from the ceiling and the capacity to hold the several thousand people who are disgorged in rapid succession when numerous flights arrive close together.

There is what appears to be an endless line of immigration stations, and Disney-style zig-zag races are in place to channel the masses of new arrivals to the numerous officers who are stationed there waiting to check and stamp passports.

The U.S. Immigration entry document is surely the most detailed of any country in the world, and the officers who police it are pernickety about how the form is completed. No strike-outs are allowed; any mistake means a new form.

Just after 6 a.m. on the day in question, four or five Jumbo flights had arrived in close succession from 'Down Under.' The arrival hall was buzzing with people, about two-thirds of whom were aliens.

Fortunately for us, we arrived on the first of these planes, and were about 10th or 12th in line in our queue. Our processing officer was definitely not a 'happy chappy' that morning, and I'm sure it would have been better if he had stayed home that day. After processing his first passenger, who had made an error in completing his form, the officer stood up and announced, or should I say yelled, to the entire area, "If anybody here fills out their form incorrectly, I'll send them to the back of the queue and they can start again. HAVE YOU ALL GOT IT?" We eventually made our way to the head of our line, and were duly summoned by this clearly angry man. "Next!"

We moved to his station, and he pointed at me and said, "You first." I gave him my passport, which he scanned. Then he said to me, "Put your left index finger on the pad." I waited several moments–you might describe it as a pregnant pause–before replying, "I don't have one of those."

My response totally rattled this fellow, who didn't know what to say. My situation was obviously not covered in the fingerprinting training manual. Just as he was starting to rise to his feet to send us to the end of the queue, I felt an amazing blow to my right ankle. For one brief moment, I thought it had been fractured. What had happened? It only took me a nanosecond to realize that my wife of thirty-eight years had just kicked me to display her deep dissatisfaction after our exhausting journey from Australia, the longest plane flight on the planet. She was tired, and definitely didn't need to be sent to the end of the queue to do it all over again.

The instant I received the blow to my ankle, I thrust my left hand out, held it right in front of the officer's face with all three fingers and thumb spread wide apart, and said, "I'm a disabled person!" In the world of political correctness in which we live today, and this being a public officer in America, I knew I was on a winner.

He didn't rise from his chair; his anger just died, and he looked like death warmed up. His brain was fried. Practitioners of Neuro Linguistic Programming call this a 'pattern interrupt.'

"Which finger do you want, sir?" I continued, at the same time wrapping my thumb around my fourth and fifth fingers, leaving only my middle finger pointing upwards in what has occasionally been described as a 'royal salute.' "This one, sir?" I said. At this moment, all the people in the long, winding queue behind us who had been observing our interaction burst into hastily covered laughter.

Our poor immigration officer was now totally confused, and way out of his depth. He had obviously never been confronted with this situation before, and was now in uncharted territory. I then wrapped my thumb around my third and fifth fingers and sent my fourth finger skyward. "Is it this finger you want, sir?" While he searched for a response, I completed the suite and raised my little finger. "Is it this finger you want, sir?" He was so rattled by now that he eventually responded, "Just give me any finger." I gave him my 'royal salute' finger and finally, the processing of my left hand was complete, however we weren't finished yet; there was still my right hand to fingerprint.

"Now the other hand," said our man. "Which finger do you want, sir?" I asked, while at the same time giving him the 'royal salute' with each finger in turn. The crowd was still giggling, enjoying the entertainment. "The right index finger," he said, glowering at me. He took my fingerprint, and finally I was done. As he stamped my passport to get rid of me and start processing Judy, I suddenly pulled out one of my "Expect a Miracle" cards and gave it to him. The look on his face turned from one of despair to one of humor when he read the words on the card.

"This is a gift from me to you, sir" I said. "You have a very difficult job dealing with all sorts of crazy people and things, don't you?" He sighed and said, "Thank you, I could often do with a miracle. Can I have this card?" "Absolutely," I said. "It's my gift to you." The officer then lightened up as he processed Judy's documents, and by the time we moved on to collect our bags, we left a smiling and now happy immigration officer to care for the other passengers. He also made certain that porters were available to help me, as I was a disabled person! The only residual effect from this encounter was my sore ankle, a gift from my unapologetic wife.

Dr. John Hinwood

Patience, persistence and perspiration make an unbeatable combination for success.

Napoleon Hill

2

MIRACLES OF COURAGE

Courage, it would seem, is nothing less than the power to overcome danger, misfortune, fear, injustice, while continuing to affirm inwardly that life with all its sorrows is good; that everything is meaningful even if in a sense beyond our understanding; and that there is always tomorrow.

Dorothy Thompson

Bowed, but not Broken

Selecting a suitable card to send was proving to be a big job for the elderly man. He was struggling on a walker, and had difficulty speaking, I presumed after a stroke. It saddened me to see him covering his crooked mouth as he strained to control his out-of-balance body, and the grimace that was his best attempt at a smile.

All I could do was maintain eye contact, smile and keep up a conversation – his mental and physical struggles were profound. And of course, give him my "business card" – an "Expect a Miracle" card. Then, he *really* chuckled. Lovely.

Dr. Judy Hinwood

When the morning's freshness has been replaced by the weariness of midday, when the leg muscles give under the strain, the climb seems endless, and suddenly nothing will be quite as you wish – it is then that you must not hesitate.

Dag Hammarskjold

Love Thy Neighbor

You never know what coming close to dying feels like, until you are there. When I was a teenager, my parents gave me and one of my brothers a ticket to go visit relatives from home as a Christmas present. We travelled to our hometown in Colombia and stayed with our aunt. My uncle was on a business trip at the time, as he was a very busy man. The first night, we were tired from our journey, and went to bed around 10 p.m.

At around 1 a.m. I was woken by repeated blows to my head with what turned out to be a gun to find that around 10 robbers had entered the house while we were all sleeping. They had bashed and tied up the maid on the first floor and put her inside a closet, unconscious. I was sleeping by myself in one of the guest bedrooms, and by the time they got to my room, everybody else had been tied up.

They then proceeded to tie me up. They kept hitting me in the head and asking me where the safe was. No matter how many times I said that I did not know, they refused to believe me, and kept hitting me with the butts of their guns. They told me that if I did not tell them, they would kill my brother. As I had no idea if there even was a safe, and so was unable to tell them where it was, they left my room and came back a few minutes later with blood all over their hands saying they had killed my brother. I was crying, and kept telling them through the socks they had stuffed in my mouth that I did not know about any safe.

Luckily, a neighbor noticed that there was a strange car parked outside and called the police before coming to our front door to check on us. The robbers heard the neighbor trying to enter the house to see if we were alright and fled before the police appeared. The police called the ambulance when they arrived and it turned out that my brother was not dead, but needed 22 stitches to close a large wound on his head. My aunt and her children were also alive, but shaken up.

That day, I realized that no matter how much you plan things in your life, sometimes there are things that just come from nowhere that turn your life upside down. The key is not to let those circumstances dictate what you become, but to rise above them and see the lesson in all that happens. The victim mentality is what causes most people to become paralyzed with who they are, and then they become fearful that it may happen again.

The key is not to shy away from difficult experiences, but to embrace them, as you will become a wiser and stronger person from them. If you truly believe that miracles can happen, then something or someone, like the neighbor who intervened to scare the robbers off, will assist you, and the miracle will happen!

Dr. Fabrizio Mancini

Courage and perseverance have a magic talisman, before which difficulties and obstacles vanish into air.

John Adams

3

MIRACLES OF FAMILY

In every conceivable manner, the family is link to our past, bridge to our future.

Alex Haley

He Ain't Heavy, He's My Brother

At the age of 67, my wife Judy visited a clairvoyant for a general chat about life, and in the course of the discussion, was told that there was a man somewhere in her life whom she should endeavor to seek out. All this was very puzzling at the time, and didn't really mean very much to Judy or me. Judy had been adopted as a three-week-old baby, and for some reason had decided, at this stage of her life, that she should explore her birth family history, however all she had to go on was her date and location of birth, and of course her adoptive mother's and father's details. I offered to assist, and started to gather records from the Registrar of Births, Deaths and Marriages, which provided some details regarding the adoption process that had occurred all those years ago.

I was able to find the birth mother's details, as well as details of who had offered Judy for adoption. We now knew that Jude's birth mother was a woman by the name of Doris Jolley. Armed with this information, I was able to search the records at the State Library, and discovered that Doris had passed away some years earlier. A search of death notices placed in the local newspaper at the time of her passing revealed one that had been placed by Doris's family indicating that, unbeknown to Jude, she had had a brother named Lawrence. Some more searching of electoral rolls, telephone directories and various other sources gave us an address for one Lawrie Wacket, the man we believed was Jude's long-lost brother. Was Lawrie really her brother? Jude wrote a letter to him outlining our discovery and offering to make contact if he chose to do so, but she fully expected that Lawrie would view the letter as an approach by some sort of crank, and discard it without any further consideration. Lo and behold, a few evenings later the phone rang. It was Lawrie, who, after introducing himself, struggled to explain his thoughts at discovering that he had a sister whom he had never known existed. The conversation went on for half an hour or so, and a meeting was arranged for a week or so later at the Cuckoo Restaurant in the beautiful Dandenong Ranges outside Melbourne.

Jude and I had a strange feeling of anticipation as we waited for Lawrie to arrive. Would he look like Jude? Was he going to be a nice person? What would his reaction to Judy be? Our questions were soon answered when Lawrie and his wife Dianne arrived with open arms and huge smiles. The next few hours were spent eagerly swapping stories of Lawrie's and Jude's respective lives, growing up, raising families, and all manner of little bits of information. It was uncanny the way in which these siblings' lives had unfolded. We have since met Lawrie and Dianne's family, and were recently honored to be invited to the christening of two of their grandchildren.

What a strange twist of fate it seems that a small comment by that clairvoyant has led to this whole new family that neither Jude nor her brother Lawrie ever knew existed...or was this a miracle?

Allan Lowe

A Gold Medal Decision

In November 1996, after completing his Higher School Certificate, our youngest son Rod received a call from the Australian Institute of Sport inviting him to take part in the trials for selection in the Australian wrestling team that would spend the next four years training for the 2000 Sydney Olympics.

Rod had only taken up wrestling three years earlier when he became a boarder at The Southport School on the Gold Coast, and he had become very good at it. Rod went to the trials, and was subsequently offered a scholarship. There was much excitement in the family, as both my wife Judy's and my first profession had been as a physical education teacher. In addition, my father had risen to become the sporting editor of the leading Sydney newspaper where he worked for more than fifty years, so sport had been a big part of our lives, and now we had a prospective Olympian in the family!

On Christmas Day of 1996, we were sitting around chatting, as families do after dinner on Christmas Day, when Rod announced that he had decided to change his goals and, instead of taking up the scholarship to attend the Australian Institute of Sport, he was going to carry on with the job he had as a trainee in a department store, save his money, and in eighteen months he would travel to Chile to look for his birth parents and any other relatives he could find.

We had adopted our three children, Shavela, Nat and Rod, who were siblings, after finding them in orphanages in Chile in 1985 when Shavela was ten, Nat was nine, and Rod was seven years old. Shavela and Nat remembered life before the orphanage, not with their father, as their parents had been separated for many years, but they remembered life on the farm with their mother. Rod, on the other hand, had for some reason, probably because of childhood trauma, forgotten everything, so all his memories were of Hogar De Minores, the orphanage where we had found them.

Now, Rod felt that, at the age of eighteen, he couldn't progress any further in life until he had achieved some closure on his past life. His brother Nat decided that if Rod was going, he was going too. Judy and I thought briefly about accompanying them, but decided that, no, it was their journey, and they needed to go alone. It was the kids' trip back to Chile, and it wasn't appropriate for us to be there.

The kids had their "Expect a Miracle" cards, and they both said, "Dad, you give these cards to everyone, we're going to use one now to find our family. We're going to go there and complete that part of our life."

Later that evening, their sister Shavela phoned and said, "Mom and Dad, the three of us have decided this is a family trip. We're all going together." Great. We sat down at a family meeting, organized a budget and figured out how much everyone would have to save. Eighteen months later, we flew from Brisbane to Santiago, Chile, and then travelled to Concepción and on to various points south and east in order to find the children's birth family.

Various people at World Vision assisted us as private individuals, rather than in an official capacity, and two of them went on a missing persons radio program that was running in Chile at the time. Over 600,000 people had gone missing during Pinoche's dictatorship, and there was no record of their whereabouts. While they were on the radio, the World Vision people asked if anyone knew the whereabouts of the children's parents, so that they could seek permission for us to visit them. Fortunately, their birth father's sister was listening to the program, heard the request, and asked her brother, who lived with her, if he would be happy for us to contact him. He said yes, and so the miracle happened.

We found the children's birth father, who then put us in contact with their birth mother, and five weeks later we rejoiced at a Yevennes Parra family gathering. Over the next three weeks we met with one hundred and twenty long-lost aunts, uncles and cousins! Expect a miracle, and it's amazing what happens!

Dr. John Hinwood

Character cannot be developed in ease and quiet. Only through experience of trial and suffering can the soul be strengthened, ambition inspired and success achieved.

Helen Keller

A Miracle Birth

Dear Dr. John,

The last time I spoke with you, I was 36 weeks pregnant, upset and worried about having a caesarean delivery due to my baby being in breech position. You assured me that things would be alright in the end, and gave me a card which said "Expect a Miracle." Well, a miracle is exactly what happened.

After having an ultrasound to confirm the breech position, I was placed under the care of the professor of obstetrics at the Mater Mothers Hospital, who was happy for me to have a vaginal breech delivery under close supervision. When I still hadn't gone into labor after 41 weeks, I was admitted to hospital to have my labor induced.

Soon after the hormone drip was started the baby's feet dropped down into the birth canal, and it looked like I would have to have a caesarean after all. They began to prep me, but fortunately the professor was there, and agreed that I could continue with a natural delivery.

I'm happy to say that after being in labor for just two and a half hours, I delivered a 6 lb 9 oz baby boy with no assistance and no complications. He emerged feet first, and had the umbilical cord wrapped tightly around his neck, but once the cord was cut he took his first breath and let out an almighty cry. We named him Joel, and he is doing very well.

So, all was indeed alright in the end, better than anyone could have dreamed. Thank you once again for the "Expect a Miracle" card and for your assurance when I was feeling down. It's nice to know that miracles do happen!

Best wishes to you and your staff,

Brenda Veenbaas

You gain strength, courage and confidence by every experience in which you really stop to look fear in the face.

Eleanor Roosevelt

4

MIRACLES
OF FREEDOM

*We seek peace, knowing
that peace is the climate
of freedom.*

Dwight Eisenhower

Cleaning Up

I have great memories of a practice development workshop I attended a number of years ago that Dr. John Hinwood was conducting. We were looking at how our attitudes to money could either hold us back or move us forward in life. It was a pretty intense session, with loads of energy in the room as some people really struggled with the concepts.

We had just completed a session on 'Release, Let Go and Move On,' and had made a big mess, having torn up paper into tiny pieces which were now strewn all over the floor like confetti. Now, John told us to stand on our chairs and pull out the largest note we had in our wallet or purse. Quite a few $50 notes were produced, as well as some $20 notes. I think there was well over $500 in total. The exercise was about 'How money can control us.' We had to trust the process, let John take the money from us, and be prepared to lose it. He took each person's note, screwed them all up, and then threw them all in the air so that they landed on the floor amongst all the rubbish.

The money was still on the floor when the conference finished. I was standing at the back of the room and saw John walk up to the cleaner who had just entered the room to do her job. He introduced himself and said, "Look, we've made quite a large mess on the floor. I really apologize for this." Then he handed the woman an "Expect a Miracle" card, which made her laugh. He then said, "Thank you very much, we don't require anything that's on the floor, so if there's anything of interest there, you can keep it for yourself." He then wished her a good night and walked out the door.

I was so intrigued by what the cleaner's reaction would be when she found the money that I stayed in the room to watch. When she walked to the front of the room and saw what was on the floor, she screamed with delight. I'm sure she knew that the "Expect a Miracle" card that John had given her had indeed delivered the miracle of all that money on the floor amongst all the confetti.

Dr. Clinton McCauley

You've got to get to the stage in life where going for it is more important than winning or losing.

Arthur Ashe

Mister Miracle Man

A number of years ago, we relocated to a new town and soon found a wonderful Asian restaurant that was owned and run by a very friendly Chinese family. When I paid for our meal on our first visit, I gave the owner one of my "Expect a Miracle" cards. Her immediate response was, "What this miracle?"

I spent the next five minutes trying to explain what a miracle was to this loving, caring Asian lady who had little English, but when I left the restaurant, I felt that I hadn't done a very good job with my attempts at an explanation, and thought that the "Expect a Miracle" card would probably end up in the rubbish bin.

A week later, my wife Judy phoned through a takeaway order that I would collect on my way home from the gym. When I entered the restaurant to collect our order, the lady I'd given the "Expect a Miracle" card to came running up to me saying, 'Thank you, thank you, thank you, Mister Miracle Man! We have a family miracle, thank you to you!"

She then insisted on taking me to every table in the restaurant, which was full, and introducing me to each individual diner saying, "This is Mister Miracle Man!" She was all smiles and enthusiasm, and very demonstrative, which is quite unusual for a Chinese lady in public. When I finally received my food, which she wouldn't allow me to pay for, this ecstatic lady gave me a bottle of very expensive champagne as a special gift.

For the next year, until they eventually sold the restaurant and moved on, the owners always greeted me as 'Mister Miracle Man' whenever we went to their restaurant. Funnily enough, to this day I have no idea what the miracle was that they experienced, for they never revealed it to me.

Dr. John Hinwood

5

MIRACLES
OF FRIENDS

*True friendship consists not in
the multitude of friends, but in
their worth and value.*

Ben Jonson

The Not-so-silly Housekeeper

I first came to work for John and Judy Hinwood in July 2006, housekeeping one day a week. It was not long before I was introduced to John and Judy's "Expect a Miracle" cards, slipped lovingly into a book they gave me as a gift.

I loved the book, but cherished my little card even more. It felt very precious, like a little piece of sunshine and hope. I made a copy of the card, so that I could carry one card in my wallet and keep another by my bedside lamp. Now, it brings a smile to my face at the start of each day.

A few weeks later, I was out with my eldest son, who is 35, my 13-year-old grandson, and my two younger children, aged 12 and 9. We were buying ice-creams and as I opened my wallet to pay, my son Kieran, who was standing alongside me, spied my "Expect a Miracle" card. "What's that?" he said. I took the card out of my wallet and handed it to him. "Here, darling. Slip it into your pocket," I said. His look of surprise and delight warmed my heart.

Two days later, he called me up. "Mom! Remember that card you gave me? I finally sold the boat yesterday! Should I pass it on now?" "No, darling, keep it," I replied. "These miracles just keep coming. You're not limited to one. Life is your oyster, and you deserve all the pearls it can produce." Since then, my son has asked for more cards so he can pass along his gift.

This year, I popped a card into each of my Christmas cards

to my dearest friends, and received phone calls of delight from many of them. Again, it was as if I'd sent each of them a fabulous gift.

I've given them to many people now, from 18-year-olds to 80-year-olds, and I always receive the same response, which is one of delight, hope, excitement and a special smile. I've even converted cynics (even if just a little).

For example, Jonathan is a friend I met when I came to housekeep for him and his wife two years ago. His wife Demi passed away with cancer just over a year later, and he had already lost his daughter Emily 10 years earlier, almost to the day. He is a very practical man who doesn't have a lot of time for "rot" (he's very, very English!).

One day, late last year, in came his 'dotty' housekeeper with a Christmas present. I had also placed an "Expect a Miracle" card on his desk, in front of his computer. After reading it, he tossed it aside in disdain (he told me later) and smiled about the 'quite mad' housekeeper he had employed.

Later in the week, as the New Year drew closer, he received a call from a friend, a woman he had known for many years. It had been 12 months since Demi's passing, and Jonathan was feeling the need for female company, however getting back into the dating game terrified him. When Kim, with whom he had had a spark brewing ever so quietly in his heart for a while now, called he thought it was too good to be true. She asked him if he would like to accompany her, along with her mother, her daughter and her granddaughter, to a New Year's Eve dinner and fireworks display.

He wrote the address on a blank card that was lying near the phone and popped it into the street directory ready for the outing the following day. He had a wonderful night with Kim and her family, and ended up staying over. As he was leaving the next morning, he moved the street directory as he got into the car, and out fell the address card onto the seat. He turned it over and read the message on the other side: "Expect a Miracle." Smiling to himself, he made a mental note to thank that silly housekeeper of his.

Two days later, he got a call from another female friend inviting him to dinner. "Well," he said "These bloody miracles just seem to keep coming – how come?"

Gayle Gibbon

> *Your chances of success are directly proportional to the degree of pleasure you derive from what you do.*
>
> *Michael Korda*

A Little Bunch
of Miracles

I've had lots of fun over the years giving "Expect a Miracle" cards to family, friends and strangers. Some of the miracles I've seen and heard about are amazing.

Seeing a light reignite in someone's eyes and a smile return to their face – simply by sharing a card and a smile – is a *big* miracle in my book! One lady called me up and said that after receiving the card, she got her old job back and restarted her life after having been through a recent tragedy. She was *very* grateful. On receiving an "Expect a Miracle" card, one gentleman screeched with delight and said it was the sign he'd been waiting for to give him the gumption to start a new career. Wow! On returning to a local Italian restaurant, we were immediately recognized and thanked by the owner, Lucas, for leaving a card last time. He said he had been overwhelmed with the pure giving as he searched for some business promotion ideas. He added that they would never do that in Italy, although I'm sure they do! A lady came back to me and asked for another "Expect a Miracle" card as she had passed hers on to her friend. She said her friend had experienced an *amazing* recovery from an illness, and had said that it was because of the card. Several people have told me they keep their "Expect a Miracle" card in a prominent place to remind them at all times that they do indeed have a miracle life!

Berni Ireland

Letter to
Dr. John Hinwood

Dear John,

RE: Thank you for your magic "Expect a Miracle" cards

John, my long-standing friend and mentor, your "Expect a Miracle" cards are *not* cards, they are gifts of miracles, and they tend to work best when a miracle is most needed. This has been my repeated personal experience, time after time!

As you would recall, I was fortunate enough to first meet you and Judy as a chiropractic patient about 23 years ago, when you were at your Underwood Chiropractic Practice. When you first handed me one of your "Expect a Miracle" cards was when I most needed to receive one. At first, I thought you must have lost your marbles and gone wacky, but John, with your permanently energetic and positive outlook on and in life, you have taught me, and you have repeatedly proven to me and my family that both you and Albert Einstein were and are right:

> *"There are only two ways to live your life. One is as though nothing is a miracle. The other is as though everything is a miracle."* —Albert Einstein

I have found that your "Expect a Miracle" cards are gifts of miracles that do indeed work when we are prepared to live

Letter to Dr. John

"as though everything is a miracle."

One series of examples I have experienced commenced late in 1999. As you know, I was involved in a major court case between one of my companies and its former patent attorneys. Less than two weeks prior to the commencement of proceedings, both our Brisbane-based lawyers and financial backer had withdrawn from the case, leaving me stranded. I had received a letter from the other party's solicitors in Sydney which I could not make any sense of, so I went to the Brisbane Law Courts library with an "Expect a Miracle" gift in my pocket. I could not find my way around the library, so I asked a distinguished-looking grey-haired gentleman if he could help me find what I was looking for. He duly obliged, and when we found it, he read it, and then asked me why I wanted this piece of law. I explained the situation, and he asked me to go and have a cuppa with him across the road. I spent the next two weeks with this very kind and helpful gentleman, David Selth, who was a retired Barrister-in-Law and spent a lot of time researching and putting together a legal argument for me to read out seeking the leave of the court for me to be allowed to represent my company.

I duly turned up in court with one of your "Expect a Miracle" gifts in my pocket. My friend Leonard Whittaker was with me, and he also had an "Expect a Miracle" gift in his pocket. Unbeknown to me, you and Judy were sitting at the back of the courtroom, no doubt with dozens of your very powerful "Expect a Miracle" gifts in your pockets, adding to the power of the two "Expect a Miracle" gifts that Leonard and I had in our pockets. When called by the judge, I stood and very nervously read David Selth's prepared script. A few minutes later, the judge granted me leave to proceed, at least for the time being, in order to commence the case. "What do I do now?" I whispered to Leonard. "I've run out of script. I don't know what to say next, or where to begin."

"Do what you do best," said Leonard. "Just get up and keep talking. If her Honor shuts you down, at least we got to sit here at the Bar table in the Federal Court of Australia this morning, and we know we have done our best! What more can we expect?" I had no answer to Leonard's response, but my knees had gone weak, and I had to use my hands to rise to my feet again. I was halfway up when you tapped me on the shoulder and said, "Ask for a 15- or 30-minute adjournment. There's a barrister sitting at the back of the room who I think will take over and represent you free of charge – no win, no pay." By this time, I was mentally blank, and I can't recall what I said to the judge, but I was granted an adjournment, which ended up lasting for two or three hours.

You later advised me that while you and Judy were sitting at the back of the courtroom waiting for proceedings to commence, Judy nudged you and whispered, "Isn't that Peter Gwozdecky?" Peter was your mate from chiropractic college days in Toronto, Canada back in the mid-1970s, and by a miracle you managed to keep Peter out of the clutches of the authorities following an amazing stunt that Peter, who was a world-class trick water-ski champion, performed behind a Toronto Island ferry boat one night. That night, Peter had said that he owed you a *big* favor, but after graduation in May 1977, you hadn't seen him again until that fateful day in the courtroom of the Federal Court of Australia some 22 years later, although you knew that he had decided to make a career change and had just become a Barrister-in-Law. You passed a card to the person sitting next to you and asked them to pass it on person-to-person until it reached Peter. I assume it was one of your "Expect a Miracle" gifts. Upon receiving your card, Peter looked around and you signaled for him to join you out in the corridor, where you explained to him that I was a friend of yours.

Peter explained that he had a small case coming up in the

Federal Court, and was there to see how that court worked. He had been expecting another case that he wanted to listen to, but he hadn't bothered to check the listing, in which case he would have found that it had been moved to another court-room, and so Peter had found himself listening to my company's case. Yet another miracle! Peter agreed to do what he could to help, and so once he had obtained an adjournment for a week or two, we took the files over to his chambers. Peter kept telling us that he was not sufficiently experienced, and did not think he would be able to be of much help to me, nevertheless, we left him with the files and the next morning I found a message on my mobile phone from Peter who said that he and a fellow barrister mate of his wanted to meet with Leonard and me as soon as possible.

We met with Peter, who introduced us to a slightly more senior barrister, Frank Santini, who had apparently been a barrister for about 6 or 12 months longer than Peter. They went back to court and obtained another adjournment until after the Christmas recess, which gave us time to find a so-licitor to help put a case together. Another miracle! Over the next few months, which included many days of very long hours that often extended into the early hours of the follow-ing morning, Frank became an appreciative convert to chiro-practic adjustments on the floor of Peter's chambers. Frank had agreed to run the case if Peter would help him, and was also acting pro bono on a no win, no pay basis. Yet another miracle!

They then introduced me to a solicitor, Mrs. Mary Salama, who also agreed to represent the company on the same terms. Yet another miracle! All of a sudden, when I needed help the most, right at the 11th hour, I had received first your gentle tap on the shoulder telling me to ask for a short adjournment and then within days a full legal team representing the com-pany pro bono!

Whilst we did not win that case, for reasons which I won't go into right now, we did succeed in achieving several miracles and great friendships for all of us who were involved with that very kind and generous legal team who came to my rescue, and in October 2007 I finally obtained a favourable ruling in relation to a subsequent independent matter, which was confirmed in January 2008. This was another miracle, and much bigger miracles are about to happen as a result of this long and arduous journey. These will continue to come in very different ways to those which we may sometimes expect, but providing we "Expect a Miracle," miracles will keep happening to help us when we live our lives "as though everything is a miracle."

John, I have also repeatedly found that whenever I am negotiating a business deal and the other person seems to be a little tense, when I hand them one of your "Expect a Miracle" gifts, they are disarmed, and are suddenly much more relaxed.

John, thanks again for introducing me to your "Expect a Miracle" gifts/cards.

Honorably and Sincerely Yours,

Kenneth-Clyde Ivory

> *No one has looked back on a life full of experiences, but many look back wishing they had had the courage to do more.*
>
> *Tim James*

6

MIRACLES OF HEALING AND HEALTH

Look to your health; and if you have it, praise God, and value it next to a good conscience; for health is the second blessing that we mortals are capable of; a blessing that money cannot buy.

Izaak Walton

Space Invaders

I recently turned 49, and all my adult life I've chosen a healthy lifestyle and diet, but several months ago, I collapsed one evening after work in my new chiropractic practice. One minute I was sitting at my desk writing a newsletter, then suddenly I heard a very loud blast of sound in my head and experienced a flash of white light that was just like what you would see if you pulled the power cord out while watching TV.

Fortunately, my new assistant, Lisa, had popped in to the practice, even though it was her day off, to check on some of her duties, and it was either sheer coincidence or a miracle that she happened to be there after 6 p.m. on a dark winter's night when I collapsed. My wife wasn't expecting me home for some time, so I may not have been found for hours. Lisa heard a loud bang, and ran into my room to see my feet protruding from behind a bench and twitching. At first she thought I was playing a prank (I'm prone to that!), but then she saw that I was lying face-down, biting my cheek and frothing at the mouth, and immediately called for an ambulance.

No, I didn't go into a tunnel of white light and meet my granny. Instead, I came to with paramedics attending to me and my trousers damp with urine. Apparently they asked me if I could tell them my children's names, and in my disoriented state I replied, "Children? What children?"

However, even before I was fully aware of what was happening, I remember saying a silent "Thank you" to God. I knew enough to be 'grateful in all things.' Then I was taken to hospital, where they confirmed that I had a brain tumor and had suffered an intracranial bleed.

Following my unexpected collapse, my great friends Drs John and Judy Hinwood sent me cards every day, each one filled with shiny "sprinkles" and a pack of their "Expect a Miracle" cards. I could have done without the sprinkles bursting out of each card I opened and going everywhere, but I really started to make use of the "Expect a Miracle" cards. I had so many of them that I gave cards away to complete strangers, but I placed quite a few of them in various locations around the house. I even affixed one to the glass of the shower screen. I placed a card beside each light switch in the house, because the phenomenon of harnessing electricity to light a home would have been considered a miracle in the time of Christ, but now we expect it! Everything's a miracle, but we don't think about it! Now, everywhere I go, I am confronted by this simple message, which has embedded itself into my subconscious mind.

So, where's my miracle? I'm not going to say that the tumor has disappeared – it hasn't, despite an initial six-week period of combined radiation and chemotherapy, and three more bursts of chemotherapy at monthly intervals since then. It's too precariously situated and tangled up to operate on, even though it's 'benign,' so it's a space invader, although it's apparently a type that could 'take off' at any time. It's no smaller today than the day it was first scanned more than six months ago, but that's okay. It can stay there for all I care, because I've got stuff to do and a family to bring up, and maybe it's good to have a little reminder of one's mortality sitting in there throughout what I expect to be a long life. It keeps me very much on purpose and tuned in to what I'm really here for. Anything to remind me of God's presence and sustenance in my life is good, I think. I don't need 'evidence' on a scan to convince me that I'm going to 'make it.'

What is a miracle, really? Is having a tumor shrunk under cell-selective chemotherapy and radiotherapy a miracle? Or is having a very happy and productive life with a tumor in your head a miracle? I like the latter. I can do all things through Him, who strengthens me, so from now on it's very much a team effort, as I leave the big picture with God, but I do my bit, too.

Why do I know I'm being looked after? Despite my collapse and diagnosis, I have never had any of the expected symptoms: headaches, nausea, vomiting, visual disturbances, poor coordination, long-term personality changes, and so on. I was just extremely tired a lot of the time before the collapse. Even after undergoing neurosurgery, wherein a plate of bone was lifted out and then replaced using 17 surgical staples, I have had no pain or adverse symptoms. I haven't needed to use a single painkiller, and for that, I'm very grateful. I'm also happier than I have been for years, even though I would say I've always been a naturally happy person.

I still have all my faculties, and that's a miracle. I can pass a battery of neurological tests for coordination, visual acuity and strength, despite the brain matter that sits just an inch beneath my frontal lobe being pushed right over to one side.

My 'battery life' is very low, though. A few hours of any activity, especially in the first few months following my collapse, would tire me right out, and I'd get agitated easily, but part of accepting a miracle is patience. For me to be 'patient and accepting' is a miracle in itself. I was always the guy drinking the cappuccino and reading the sports news while he drove around planning his next big project.

If an outsider was to look at our position, they would likely conclude that the last year has been 'awful' for me and my wife, as we had several mortgaged properties, large debts, and a dwindling income stream to deal with while my tumor grew and my energy levels sank. Then, six months ago, it went from 'awful' to 'really awful' with my collapse while the wolves were snapping at the door. My wife was pregnant throughout this whole ordeal with our fifth child, but fortunately, she's an amazing woman.

We have been sustained through all this, emotionally, practically and financially by fellow school parents who made us dinners, chiropractic friends who voluntarily ran my practice, and a whole host of people who deposited financial gifts into either our bank account or our letterbox! We felt very much loved, much more than I had ever previously been aware, and for that, I'm extremely grateful.

When it seemed like things were at their lowest ebb, we won an all-expenses-paid trip for two, with inner-city hotel accommodation, to a corporate box at the Australian Tennis Open. God had to be in on that! Then, just before Christmas, I landed a contract with a publisher in Germany for a book I'd written on athletics training, so I'm very grateful for that. Then to top things off, Mietta, our beautiful, healthy baby daughter was born on January 4, meaning we've now been blessed with five beautiful children. There's so much to be grateful for – you just have to go looking!

The key to expecting a miracle is to be grateful in all things! Would you give something to someone who was ungrateful? No way! God gives freely to grateful recipients, so be grateful and expect a miracle!

Dr. Keith Livingstone

Energy and persistence conquer all things.

Benjamin Franklin

The Power That Made the Body Heals the Body

It had been a beautiful summer day in Northern Ontario, and having spent the day working outside at our summer home, I went to bed early, somewhat exhausted, however my 14-year-old son Christopher and his friend Mathew stayed up. Soon after I went to bed, I was woken by two blasts that sounded like fireworks exploding, but being in somewhat of a stupor, I didn't think much about it and immediately went back to sleep. As my neighbor was to tell me later, twenty to thirty seconds later there was another blast, this time followed by a sound that woke me immediately: "Help, I can't see!"

Any parent will tell you that they can recognize the sound of their child's voice in an instant. I jumped out of bed and ran toward the sound of Christopher's screaming at the edge of the lake. Seeing my son's face on fire, I immediately threw him into the lake. Christopher and Mathew had been messing with a firecracker that was supposed to deliver a twin blast, which was what had initially woken me, but as Christopher had bent over to pick up the casing, with the intention of dipping it into the water as a safety precaution, there had been a third blast, resulting in second and third degree burns to his face and burns to both his eyes.

I packed his face in ice from the cooler that was on the deck in preparation for a family gathering the following day and we rushed to the hospital. As Chris lay on the gurney, severely burned and blind in both eyes, he said, "Dad, can you please adjust me?" In that moment, I realized what he was asking me, and the impact that would have on his recovery. Even though I had practiced chiropractic for more than 20 years, and had adjusted tens of thousands of people, in this moment of crisis I had forgotten that "The Power that made the body heals the body," and it took my son to remind me.

I palpated his neck, adjusted a very subluxated atlas (the 1st bone in the neck, just below the skull) and continued to check him every hour or so for several days. He was in pain from the burns, and the physicians did what they could to make him comfortable. Within hours we were flying to the Hospital for Sick Children in Toronto, where he was examined by an ophthalmologist who said that he might or might not regain his sight; we simply had to wait it out.

The following day, a team of plastic surgeons examined Christopher, and the prognosis was good, even though his nose looked like the end of a burned hot dog. He would need two or three skin grafts, but he was young, and recovery would likely leave him with minimal scarring, if any. The doctors suggested that I take him out of the hospital, so we checked in to The Park Hyatt in Toronto for the week.

Christopher slept most of the time, often moaning and groaning, while I pretty much stayed awake, grabbing moments rather than hours of sleep. I continued to check him, and the subluxation that had been evident the first time I had checked him seemed to be continuously present, so I adjusted him repeatedly. On the third day, he suddenly said, "Dad, are you wearing a blue shirt?" (As I write this, seven years later, my eyes are filled with tears.) As the day progressed, he told me that he could see shadows, and the next day he asked to watch television.

Nine days after the accident, we returned to the Hospital for Sick Children to see the plastic surgeons again. The young female doctor, who had been very kind during our previous

70

visit, walked into the room, took one look at Chris and said very loudly, "What have you done to him?" I was taken aback. "What do you mean?" I asked. "Look at his new skin!" she replied. "This is beautiful. What have you been giving him? What have you been putting on the burns?" "Nothing," I said. "I've been keeping the area clean, like you suggested, removing dead tissue with a Q-tip, but nothing else." "This is amazing," she replied. "He won't need any grafts if he keeps healing this way. I've never seen this before."

At that point, I explained what I had been doing, telling her that I had been adjusting my son almost every hour on the hour for the last nine days and that his subluxation pattern had been slowly normalizing, allowing his body to heal as it was designed to do. "You see, the Power that made the body heals the body," I said. She was in disbelief, but as we discussed anatomy and neurophysiology she became somewhat convinced that what I was saying was possible; it was just that it was outside her sphere of experience and expertise. Because she could not explain it, she was in awe and, even though my chiropractic experience allowed me to believe it, I too was in awe of the mysterious capacity of the human body to heal such severe wounds.

Fortunately, because of Christopher's upbringing regarding chiropractic, he had made the fateful request, "Dad, can you adjust me?" In less than four weeks, Christopher's facial burns had disappeared. His body had produced new skin cells and no evidence of the incident remained, other than a tiny scar the size of a pinhead which remains just underneath his nose to this day. Was this a miracle? Was this chiropractic in action? Was this the human body and innate intelligence in action? As described in chiropractic, the body has the innate ability to heal, provided there is no interference with transmission of this innate energy across the nervous system.

The Power That Made the Body Heals the Body

When Chris's nervous system was clear and free of interference, 'the Power that made his body healed his body,' plain and simple.

If your body is subluxated, and your nervous system is not functioning at optimum capacity, just imagine what chiropractic can do for you. You don't have to be burned or in crisis to benefit from chiropractic. Everyone should be checked regularly for subluxation, and adjusted when necessary. It's not about pain, it's about function.

Christopher was not adjusted because he had spinal pain; he was adjusted because there was evidence of subluxation in his neck, and therefore the flow of healing energy was impeded. As a result of chiropractic, he was able to heal as his body was designed to heal. What a gift. This true story is dedicated to all those who have yet to discover that 'the Power that made the body heals the body.'

Dr. Gilles Lamarche

Few men during their lifetime come anywhere near exhausting the resources dwelling within them. There are deep wells of strength that are never used.

Richard Byrd

Touched by
the Pharaohs

For as long as I can remember, I have had a back problem. We were on a lecture tour, sailing along the Nile, and by the time we reached Dendera, I felt I could go no further, but we were going to visit the Temple of Hathor, which I really wanted to see, so I persisted.

I made it to the Temple, and had a wonderful experience. The columns in this temple are twenty-seven feet high and twelve feet around the base, which is two feet thick. I sat down at the base of one of these columns and said quietly, "Now Pharaoh spirits, if you are here, please give me a miracle healing of my painful back." I closed my eyes and took a deep breath, and suddenly the heads and shoulders of two Pharaoh figures appeared. They turned slowly to face each other, and their foreheads touched gently for a second or so before they faded away. To the left of where they had been was the head and shoulders of another figure, who gave a slight, knowing smile before she too faded away.

I stood up, and was amazed to discover that my backache was gone! I hurried to catch up with my husband and the rest of the group, and I was able to complete our tour free of pain. Now and again I get a slight ache, but nothing as severe as previously. There had been times when I had been confined to bed for several days.

I believe we all have guardian angels watching over us who will help us with miracles if we ask them.

Thanks for the "Expect a Miracle" card you sent me, Dr. John. I'm keeping it in a safe place!

Joan Smith

Instead of waiting for someone to take you under their wing, go out there and find a good wing to climb under.

Dave Thomas

7

MIRACLES OF HOPE

The grand essentials of happiness are; something to do, something to love, and something to hope for.

Allan K Chalmers

Life is a Bowl of Chilli Con Carne

It was late at night, and we were at Los Angeles International Airport, on the way back to Australia after speaking at a seminar in the U.S. Most of the restaurants were closing up, however the Mexican restaurant in the self-serve area was open, so I joined the line to buy something for my wife Judy and myself to eat. While I was waiting, I got talking to the gentleman behind me in the queue, who was also on his way home. He had retired six months earlier from a major U.S. automobile corporation after thirty years as an expert on corporate restructuring and change management. One of the people he had trained at the corporation now had a major consulting business in the U.S., and as soon as this gentleman had retired from the auto corporation, his former colleague had asked him to do some consulting work. "Would you like to come and eat with us?" I said. "Sure," he replied.

When I paid for my order, I gave the Mexican lady behind the counter an "Expect a Miracle" card. "What is this card, Sir?" she said. "This is a card for you," I replied. "There must be a miracle you want today, and this will help you receive it." She looked at the card, then back at me and said, "Sir, I know it will. Thank you, sir, thank you." She then took the card and showed the other people behind the counter and out in the kitchen. It was 11.30 p.m., and we could see that the Mexicans running this food outlet had had a long day, and were very tired, but the "Expect a Miracle" card brought new life to them. Then others wanted one, of course, so I passed some more cards out. The gentleman I had invited to dine with us had seen all this of course, and said to me, "Hey, this is a great card." "Would you like one?" I said. "Oh yes!" he replied, so I gave him a card as well.

Two days later, I received an email from him, in which he said that he had been going home to commit suicide that night, as his wife of 35 years had left him a couple of weeks earlier, and his life was now a total disaster. "When I saw what that card did for those people behind the counter at the airport doing menial work, and they got really excited at the mere thought of a miracle happening, I said to myself, look at the life you have had. Look at the life you are having now. Expect a miracle, and life will change. This brought about a huge change in my thinking, in how I saw life. I can't believe that something as simple as "Expect a Miracle" written on a card can do that. All I can do is say thank you, thank you, thank you for giving me my life back. It's so simple. My miracle has arrived!"

Dr. John Hinwood

Life is something like this trumpet. If you don't put anything in it, you don't get anything out.

W C Handy

The Show Must Go On

Being in a hit show on the West End can be the fulfilment of a life-long ambition for a musical theatre artist, but all shows close eventually, sometimes earlier than hoped! It can be an anxious time between jobs, and so it was for our daughter Vivien.

Not knowing what more to say by way of encouragement, I simply placed one of John Hinwood's "Expect a Miracle" cards in an envelope and sent it to Viv. She was delighted to receive the card, and immediately stuck it on her bed head and went to sleep.

The very next day, she received the long-awaited call from her agent for the audition she had been hoping for. She was off and running again, with all her enthusiasm restored, and has continued to act in London's West End and at the famous Edinburgh Festival in Scotland.

"'Empowering' and 'liberating' were words that came to mind upon receiving the card," Viv said later. We love the 'everything is possible' message that these cards bring.

Jennifer Carter

Small opportunities are often the beginning of great enterprises.

Demosthenes

My Miracle Mother

It's a miracle that I even entered this world in the first place. My parents, Ivy and Jack, had to expect a miracle in order to have me. The birth of my sister Diana, who is six years older than me, had already proven to be a difficult enough challenge for them.

During World War II, whenever my father was on leave in Melbourne, he would travel back to Sydney, and he and my mother would attempt to produce a second child, without success. Several times they were able to conceive, but just a few weeks into her pregnancy, the longest period being a couple of months, my mother would miscarry, and they would have to start the process all over again.

After the war ended in 1945, my mother eventually become pregnant once again. My father had now returned home from his duties as an instructor in the Royal Australian Air Force, and so the doctor suggested that my mother needed to have almost constant bed rest from her fourth month onwards to minimize the chances of yet another miscarriage.

In the last few months of her pregnancy, she was confined to bed, and the doctors also inserted a device into her vagina to jam the cervix so it could not activate prematurely to bring about a spontaneous abortion of the fetus. Fortunately, it worked, and on August 31 1946, in the first year of the Baby Boomers, I entered the world.

It was an absolute miracle for my parents that they actually had their second child, and for the doctors that my mother went to term, and from that point onwards, my parents knew that anything was possible. They were real miracle thinkers, people who never looked at things in a negative manner, especially my mother. She was probably the most positive person I've ever known. She was an amazing woman who would buy small businesses that were bankrupt, build them up into very successful enterprises, and then sell them for a handsome profit and move on. I remember that her first business was a delicatessen, followed by a sandwich bar and then a card shop. She always expected that a miracle would occur that would assist her on her road forward. My father, on the other hand, didn't necessarily expect miracles to start with, but because my mother continued to produce them through her thought patterns and the positive way she lead her life, he joined in and supported her.

It was a joy to have that kind of support. I was completely knock-kneed as a very young child, and when I ran, I sometimes fell flat on my face. My parents were told, "This boy will probably end up in a wheelchair. He may not be able to walk. He has real problems, but there's nothing we can do about it." I was taken to see the great orthopedic surgeon Dr. Hugh Barry in Sydney and, with perseverance, dedication and nightly leg braces, my problems were eventually overcome. Once again, my parents expected a miracle; they expected that something different would happen. Miracle thinking has been a part of my life, a big part of my life, ever since.

Dr. John Hinwood

Making a success of the job at hand is the best step toward the kind you want.

Richard Byrd

8

MIRACLES OF LESSONS IN LIFE

The personal life deeply lived always expands into truths beyond itself.

Anais Nin

Mad Dogs and Texan Cowboys

One of my most significant hidden blessings came to me while I was in first grade. This is when and where I was told that I would be unable to learn how to read and comprehend. I was a left-handed dyslexic, and like most people at that time, my teacher knew little about 'learning disabilities.' I started in the general reading class, then I was put into a remedial reading class, and finally I was stuck in the dunces class. The only other person in this class was 'Darryl the dunce.' At times I was made to sit in the corner wearing a conical dunce's cap on my head. I felt ashamed, different and rejected, but today, I have been blessed to be able to turn what was once a dunce's cap of shame into a wizard's hat of honor.

One day, my teacher had my parents come in to the classroom, and said to them, in front of me, "Mr. and Mrs. Demartini, your son has a learning disability. I'm afraid he will never read, write, or communicate normally. I wouldn't expect him to do much in life, and I don't think he'll go very far. If I were you I would put him into sports." I remember sitting there and hearing what she was saying, and while I didn't fully understand the significance of her words, I did sense my parents' despair and uncertainty. Often, the greatest void in your life becomes your greatest value. That which you perceive as most missing or lacking in your life becomes most important, and ensures that you go out and achieve or fulfil it, but more of that later.

I had been told I would never read, write or communicate, and that I had a learning disability, so I went into sports and eventually dropped out of school early in my teenage years. The sport I really developed a love for was surfing, and at the age of 14 I left home and set out on a journey to become a globe-trotting surfer. I went to my father and said, "I'm going to California to go surfing, Dad."

He looked me in the eye and sensed that I was sincere, and that no matter what he said I was going to do it, because that was where I belonged.

"Are you capable of handling whatever happens?" he said. "Are you willing to take responsibility for whatever comes along?"

"Yes, I am," I replied.

"I'm not going to fight you, son," he said. "You have my blessings." Then he prepared a notarized letter saying, "My son is not a runaway. He's not a vagrant. He's a boy with a dream." My mom and dad gave me a ride to the freeway and said, "Go follow your dreams, son."

Years later, I found out that when my dad came back from World War II he had hoped to go to California, but never made it. Parents often live vicariously through their children, and their kids can help heal them by living their unfulfilled dreams in their own way. When he heard me say I was going to California, I believe his old dream came back to him and he thought, well, I never made it, but I'm not going to stop you, son.

My First Mentor
I set off to hitchhike to California, and eventually came to El Paso, Texas. I was walking along a downtown sidewalk when I saw three cowboys ahead of me. I wore a headband and was growing my hair long, because that was the thing to do in the sixties if you were a surfer, and in those days, cowboys and

surfers didn't get along. There was a simmering, ongoing war between the shorthaired rednecks and longhaired white-necks. As I walked down that sidewalk with my long hair, backpack and surfboard, I knew I was about to be confronted by an obstacle.

I knew that they would likely beat me up and leave me lying hurt in the street. I didn't know what to do. As I approached them, they lined up across the sidewalk and just stood there with their thumbs in their belts. They clearly weren't going to let me through. I was thinking, "What am I gonna do? Oh God, what am I gonna do?" All of a sudden, my inner voice spoke to me. That was the first time I had been aware of my inner voice.

My intuition spoke to me, and it told me to…bark! Now, that may not have been the most inspired thing for my inner voice to say, but so what. It had said to bark, so I just went along with it.

"Ruff! Ruff! Raaarrrruff!" I went. Lo and behold, the cowboys, who were probably thinking, "This kid is nuts," all stepped aside out of my way! That was when I learned that if I trusted my intuition, amazing things would happen. So often, it is in times of perceived adversity and challenge that the greatest leaps forward are made. It is in these moments that we're taken out of our comfort zones, and we discover that we are more than we ever knew.

As I walked safely beyond the three cowboys, I felt like I had just come out of some form of trance. I turned and gave them one last bark, and then turned away from them and kept walking. When I reached the next street corner, there, leaning on a lamppost, laughing his rear end off, was a bum. He was a bald-headed old coot in his sixties or so with about four days worth of stubble, and he was laughing so hard he had to hang on to the lamppost to hold himself up.

"Sonny," he said, "That's the funniest dang thing I've ever

seen. You took care of them cowpokes like a pro!" He put his hand on my shoulder and walked me down the street. This bum was to become my first mentor.

"Can I buy you a cup of coffee?" he said.

"No sir, I don't drink coffee."

"Well, can I buy you a coke?"

"Yes sir!" and so I walked with my new-found mentor up to a little malt shop with the swivel stools along the counter.

We took a seat and he said, "So, where are you headed to sonny?"

"I'm going to California."

"Are you a runaway?"

"No, my parents gave me a ride to the freeway."

"You dropped out of school?"

"Well, yeah. I was told I would never read, write or communicate, so I just went into sports."

"Are you finished with your coke?" he said.

"Yep."

"Follow me, young man."

So I followed this scruffy old man, who took me a few blocks down the street, and then a few blocks more, until finally he led me through the front doors of the El Paso Downtown Library.

"Put your stuff down here. It'll be safe," he said. We walked on into the library, and he sat me down at a table. "Sit down, young man. I'll be right back," and off he went in among the bookshelves.

A few minutes later, he returned with a couple of books, and sat down next to me.

"There are two things I want to teach you, young man, two things I don't want you to ever forget. You promise?"

"Yes sir, I do."

"Number one, young fella, is never judge a book by its cover."

"Yes sir."

"You probably think I'm a bum, but let me tell you a little secret. I'm one of the wealthiest men in all of America. I come from the north-east, and I have every single thing that money has ever been able to buy. I have the cars, planes and houses, but a year ago, someone very dear to me passed away, and when she went, I reflected on my life and thought, 'I have everything except one experience. What's it like to have nothing, and to live on the streets?'

"So I made a commitment to travel around America from city to city with nothing, just so I had that experience before I died. So son, don't you ever judge a book by its cover, because it will fool you."

Then he grabbed my right hand, pulled it forward and set it on top of the two books that he had placed on the table. They were the works of Aristotle and Plato.

Then, he said to me with such intensity and clarity that I've never forgotten it, "You learn how to read, boy. You learn how to read, 'cause there's only two things that the world can't take away from you, and that's your love and your wisdom. So you learn how to read, boy, and grow your love and wisdom. They can take away your loved ones, they can take away your money, they can take away just about everything, but they can't take away your love and your wisdom. You remember that, boy."

"Yes sir, I will," I said.

And then he sent me on my way to California. To this day, I have never forgotten his message, that love and wisdom are the essence of our life. That has now become the core of The Breakthrough Experience™. Love and wisdom are the essence of life, and they cannot be lost.

Dr. John Demartini

Waste Not Want Not

Normally, we have 3,000 to 5,000 "Expect a Miracle" cards printed every year. I give them to people everywhere I go, my wife Judy hands them out, and our team members also hand them out.

On one occasion, I engaged a new printer to print another batch of cards, and when I returned to collect them, I found that instead of the cards being printed on nice, shiny, double-coated 350 gsm board, they had been printed on 125 gsm stock, which is just thick paper. "Pardon me," I said to the lady behind the counter, "there's been a mistake here. My order stated that these cards were to be printed on good, thick board, just like this card I have in my hand." There were four or five customers in the shop at the time, all waiting to be served, and this lady was obviously stressed. She exploded, and started to scream at me, saying I had to take them. "No, pardon me," I said, "this is what the order says. It specifies the 350gsm board. This is not that board. I need them re-done, thank you."

After a lot more screaming and yelling, she reluctantly agreed that they would have to reprint my cards on the correct stock, and then flung the boxes of misprinted cards at me and said, "I don't want them. They're yours, take them!" I left the store knowing I couldn't use these cards. Now what? The Salvation Army is always handing out care packages to people, I thought. Perhaps they could slip one of these cards into each parcel. I went to see the Captain at the local Salvation Army premises and said, "There's been an error at the printers. I can't use these, and the printer doesn't want them, so I would like to give them to you. These are courtesy of the printing company." "Wow," he said. "What are the owners' names? I'd like to send them a thank you note." I gave him the lady's name, and said, "Great, would you like to write your thank you note and then send it to me, and when I go in to pick up my reprinted cards, I can give it to her."

About a week later, I received a letter from the Salvation Army Captain in which he had enclosed a beautiful thank you note about what these cards were doing in changing people's lives in the community. When I went to collect my reprinted cards, I said to the lady, "This letter is from the Captain of the Salvation Army. He was extremely appreciative of those cards that I couldn't use." I then passed her the letter, which she read before bursting into tears. Between sobs, she said, "I'm so sorry for how I acted." "That's not a problem," I said. "I understand. Life happens, and we all have good days and some less than good days. Thank you for giving those cards to me and not throwing them in the bin, because they've now had the opportunity to be so useful and have affected the lives of many people in such a positive way." A lovely result all round.

Dr. John Hinwood

Fix the problem, not the blame.

Japanese Proverb

Mister Barrelguts

U p until the latter stages of the 20th century, corporal punishment, using either the cane or a strap, for misdemeanors by boys was acceptable in Australian schools. I can still remember, and feel, the outcome of poor due diligence on my part on my first day of secondary school in January 1959.

As I was dyslexic (a condition that was little understood in those days) I didn't do too well in primary school, and was deemed as being unable to cope with high school, so I was sent to a secondary technical school, where I was to be given a basic education before being sent out into the workforce, with or without an Intermediate Certificate, at 15 years of age.

In primary school, my dyslexia meant I often had to ask my fellow classmates for clarification or help with something I didn't understand, which meant that I was often caned for talking or being disruptive.

My problem did have one advantage, in that I developed a memory like a steel trap, so that once I learnt something, I never forgot it. This meant that I could be sent to deliver messages around the school, because the teachers were pretty sure I would deliver the message correctly. Since I spent quite a bit of time sitting outside either our classroom or the headmaster's office for being disruptive, I was often used as a messenger boy.

On my first day of secondary school, the deputy headmaster, Mr. Kelly, came into our math class and asked could he please have a boy who was good at running messages. As soon as I heard the words "good at running messages" I thrust up my hand, beamed a happy smile and said, "Pick me, Sir." My enthusiasm secured the job for me. I was so proud of myself. It was just the first hour of secondary school, and I had been the first boy to be picked to run messages.

Mr. Kelly gave me the written message to take to Mr. Kennedy, who was a woodwork teacher, I was told. He occupied a small, portable building on the far north-western boundary of the school grounds.

I was to learn later that Mr. Kennedy specialized in teaching General Activity (GA) classes. These were for boys of very limited intelligence who found even basic primary school-level English and math to be a major challenge, and manual subjects were their saving grace. These GA boys were invariably the school troublemakers, as some were petty criminals on bonds, and others were downright thugs.

Unbeknown to me at the time of delivering this message, Mr. Kennedy was a very distinctive individual. He was in his mid-sixties, of medium height, wore thick horn-rimmed glasses and weighed well over 300 pounds. He was gruff, poorly shaven (most unusual in those days), wore a grey dust-coat with wood-glue stains all over it, had breath which smelt like over-cooked cabbage and always had a well-worn felt hat on his head, whether he was inside or out. Due to his excessive weight, the boys' nickname for him was 'Mister Barrelguts.'

When I arrived at the woodwork room, there were four boys standing outside. They had been thrown out of class by Mr. Kennedy for inappropriate behavior and were now whiling away the time out in the yard. These boys, who looked to be about fourteen, were just filling in time until they were fourteen years and ten months old, at which time they would finally be able to leave school.

I was just about to knock on the door when I suddenly realized I had forgotten the teacher's name. Being totally naïve, twelve years old, and having come from a small primary school where I had been 'cock of the walk,' I wasn't aware that boys might tell you an untruth when asked a question.

When I asked these boys, "What's your teacher's name, please?" the four of them immediately replied, "Mr Barrelguts."

I knocked on the door, and a gruff voice yelled, "Come in." I opened the door, and saw a dozen boys working away at woodwork benches, and the teacher standing next to one of them. "What do you want boy?" I should also mention that I was a stutterer of note when I was nervous back in those days. "I ha-a-ve a no-no-note fo-fo-for you, M-M-M-Mister B-B-B-Barrelguts."

It transpired that he knew he'd had this nickname for many years, and he hated it, however no one had ever called him 'Mister Barrelguts' to his face before. The next thing I knew, all hell had broken loose. The boys in the room all burst out in an uproar of laughter, and steam seemed to emerge from Mr. Kennedy's nose and ears as he quickly assumed the appearance of a very angry dragon.

His immediate reaction to my innocent greeting was to scream at the boys, who were doubled over laughing. "Shut up, shut up, shut up you idiots!" Then he roared at me, "Get over here, boy!" The next few minutes were a whirlwind. His fury was frightening. "Get over into that open space and put your right hand out," he barked. Then he reached behind a tall cupboard and pulled out the longest, fattest cane I had even seen. I had been used to being caned in primary school for talking and being disruptive, usually one cut, and occasionally two cuts. Once, I had received four cuts from the headmaster after being involved in a fight, but I had never received six cuts, the known maximum; only a boy who had been expelled from the school had ever received six cuts.

Mister Barrelguts

As he raised the cane for the first time, Mr. Kennedy screamed at me, "I'm going to give you eight cuts, you ignoramus!" 'Swish' went the cane, and I felt a blow that was far more severe than anything I had ever received in primary school. "Put the other hand out!" he screamed. 'Swish' went the cane again as I received cut number two. On his fifth stroke, I pulled my hand back just before the cane made contact with my now stinging hand. That proved to be a big mistake on my part, as he was very fast and adept with the 'waddy,' and slammed my knuckles on the way back up as I put my hand out again. This reverse strike broke the skin, and my knuckles started to bleed. I realized it would be best to take the remaining cuts on my fingers and palms. After the eighth stroke of the cane, Mr. Kennedy was huffing and puffing and very red in the face, as if he was about to blow a gasket. "Now get out of here, and never ever speak to me like that again, boy. I'll remember you!" he snarled. Bruised, battered and bleeding, I made my way back to my classroom.

When I arrived home that afternoon, my father asked me what I had learnt from receiving those eight cuts of the cane. I still remember telling him that I learnt that other people don't always tell you the truth when you ask for some information. He then asked me what else I had learnt. My answer was that I would never, ever get the cane again at school. I would move forward.

This episode resulted in some miracles happening for me in my life from there on. Taking those eight cuts of the cane without crying elevated me in the minds of those delinquent boys as someone who had some 'guts' and they left me alone after that. I never did receive the cane again in my school career, and it also did something else for me. It started a process that saw my stuttering improve from marked to quite a manageable level over the next two years, and at the start of my third year at the school, I was named School Captain and

Head Prefect. Mr. Kennedy even became my rugby league coach in my second year, and he appointed me Captain of the Under-14s A team.

My resolution stuck, and the new path this incident had set me on saw me become the Athletics Champion, Swimming Champion, Dux of the School and also the winner of the Citizenship and Leadership Award in my final year. I still have the Parker fountain pen, in its inscribed case, that I was presented with at the school's speech day in 1961, not a bad result after such a troubled start to my secondary schooling.

Dr. John Hinwood

To be a leader, you have to make people want to follow you and nobody wants to follow someone who doesn't know where he is going.

Joe Namath

9

MIRACLES
OF LOVE

Love at first sight is easy to understand; it's when two people have been looking at each other for a lifetime that it becomes a miracle.

Amy Bloom

An Action Moment

Sometimes a 'moment' so obviously needs an action.

As I walked by the $2 shop, I saw a young, sad girl leaning on her cash register. She was obviously fighting back tears, so I took a couple of paces in her direction and embraced her in a gentle hug. The tears flowed, and no words were needed. I placed an "Expect a Miracle" card on her cash register, which stemmed the tears. A small bunch of flowers that I picked up from a nearby florist reduced her to tears again, but this time it was tears of happiness.

An hour later, I happened to walk by again, and this time the young girl nodded slightly to me while she worked, and I raised an eyebrow in return. Then we both smiled. She had made my day.

Dr. Judy Hinwood

Service to others is the rent you pay for your room here on earth.

Muhammad Ali

The Love of a Mother

When we think back over our lives, we can often see how they could have taken a totally different direction. The words that others say to us, particularly in our early years, can have a great impact on our direction in life, whether positive or negative.

When I was a high school student in Canada, I found school very challenging. I went to one of the toughest high schools, academically, in Toronto, and felt intimidated by the other bright students in my classes. When I failed grade 12, my parents decided to take me to a psychologist to evaluate my capabilities. After two days of intensive aptitude tests, the psychologist sat me and my parents down and said something I remember to this day.

"Mr and Mrs Lazar, after two days of testing, I have determined that Ely just doesn't have the capacity to go much further. He will be lucky to pass grade 12 the second time around, so you can forget about grade 13 (we had 13 grades in the province of Ontario, and grade 13 was the path to university), and university is just totally out of the question." Now receiving this sort of news can be devastating, in fact I sunk down into my chair when I heard what she said. The psychologist suggested that I might be able to get by at a trade school, which my father immediately wanted me to pursue, however my mother said, "I don't believe what these tests are saying. I know my son can do much better." With much coaxing from my mother, my father agreed to let me have another go at grade 12.

I managed to pass grade 12 the second time around, and I

also managed to pass grade 13, and my marks were just high enough for me to be accepted into a Bachelor of Science program at the University of Toronto. By my 3rd year at university, I was scoring a B average. I was then accepted into chiropractic college, where I continued to excel academically, scoring an A average over the four years of the course. I realized then that in high school, I hadn't been doing what I loved, and no one had been able to explain to me why doing well in high school should be high on my list of priorities. Once I got into university, and then chiropractic college, I was starting to study what I loved.

I really have to thank my mother for staying strong, because intuitively she knew that I had the capacity to do well. The love of a mother can be a powerful factor in moulding a child's future. She never knew how powerful her belief in me was!

Dr. Ely Lazar

Excellence is the gradual result of always striving to do better.

Pat Riley

It's Working Señor, It's Working!

A couple of years ago, my wife Judy and I were in London to present one of our seminars to European chiropractors and to visit our youngest son, who had moved there from Australia three years earlier. On the Sunday after the seminar, our son Rod, his partner Beth, Judy and I had a day walking around exploring London. At around 2 p.m. we all decided we were hungry, and Rod and Beth knew of a great Nando's restaurant in the area that had the most outstanding chilli and herb flame-grilled chicken.

On arriving at the restaurant we joined the queue just inside the front door and were told by the greeter that it would be about a forty-five minute wait for a table. As it had just started raining, we thought a forty-five minute wait in a dry and warm environment was far better than searching for another eatery in the rain. As is my custom, I handed our Hispanic greeter an "Expect a Miracle" card and told him that I was sure folks would leave sooner than he thought, so we were happy to wait in line for a table to become vacant. I asked him for his name, and he said it was José, and that he was from El Salvador. José then asked me if the "Expect a Miracle" card could help him to get anything he wanted in life. My answer, as always, was "Absolutely!" If your intention is extremely strong and you expect a miracle to happen, it so often does. I told him of William Allen's statement, "What the mind of man can see and believe, it can achieve."

José then started to get noticeably excited, and I asked him what the miracle was that he was seeking. "Señor, I can't tell you with ladies here," he replied, so I encouraged him to whisper it in my ear. He came close to me and whispered,

"Señor, you see that beautiful waitress over there? She's hot! I really want that hot chick!" I kept listening as he went on to explain that she didn't know he was alive, and had not responded to his approaches and advances in the past.

I assured José that with the "Expect a Miracle" card in his pocket, his wish could come true. He only had to go for it. Off he went to attend to his duties, and ten minutes later he returned with a gift of a special antipasto plate for the four of us to nibble on while we waited for a table. On presenting us with the plate of food, he also shared his excitement with me. "It's working Señor, it's working!" he enthused. I discreetly shared his wish with Judy, Beth and Rod, and we all smiled at each other and observed José's antics as he strutted his stuff for the 'hot chick.' It was fun to watch.

A table became available after just thirty minutes, and José would return every ten minutes or so to report back to me on his progress. Each time he returned, his, "It's working, Señor, it's working!" was more passionate. We all had an exceptional lunch that day, a fun experience and a special family time together, as well as seeing those three magic words, "Expect a Miracle" bring joy to José's life in London, his new-found home.

Dr. John Hinwood

You can't wait for inspiration, you have to go after it with a club.

Jack London

10

MIRACLES
OF SELF

I prefer to be true to myself, even at the hazard of incurring the ridicule of others, rather than be false, and to incur my own abhorrence.

Frederick Douglas

A Nutty Story

Late one Saturday afternoon, during my days at teachers training college studying physical education, I was heading out to a party after our rugby union game. It was around 5.30 p.m. and the sun was setting as I drove past Calam Park Mental Hospital in Sydney when I suddenly felt the unmistakable signs of a flat tire. I wasn't very happy as I pulled over, got out of the car and proceeded to set about changing the tire. I found the wrench, removed the wheel nuts and put them inside the hubcap to make sure that I didn't lose them, but while I was removing the flat tire, it slipped and landed on the edge of the hubcap, flipping the nuts out. I had pulled over right next to a grate over a drain, and before I had a chance to react, all the nuts disappeared through the grate and down into the drain. The nuts were gone forever, and I was hopping mad.

Where, on a Saturday evening, was I going to find someone to bring me a set of wheel nuts? I was not a happy chappy at all, and was cursing my luck when suddenly, I heard a voice from somewhere behind me saying, "Mate, I know how you can fix that." I turned around and saw a man standing on the other side of a large wire fence. "What would you know about this?" I snapped. I was very cross. "Well, I'll tell you what mate," he said, "you go round and you take one nut from each of the three good wheels. Then at least you'll have three nuts on that wheel, and if you put them on in the shape of a triangle that will hold it on perfectly. The other wheels will still have four nuts, so they'll be okay. That'll be good enough until you can go and get some more wheel nuts tomorrow."

A Nutty Story

"Mate, that's brilliant, fantastic," I said. "I'm really sorry I spoke harshly to you. I take it all back, mate. You're a star, you're brilliant, you're a miracle man!" "You know what mate," he said, "when they put us in here, we're all crazy, and we all know that mate, but there's one thing we definitely aren't, and that's stupid." I'd been saved by an inmate in a mental institution!

That 'miracle' story has stayed in my mind ever since that day and I know that if you want to achieve something, it can sometimes help to be a little crazy, out there, on the edge, thinking differently, thinking laterally, thinking outside the box. Just because you're crazy definitely doesn't mean you're stupid. It's a great lesson.

Dr. John Hinwood

Iron rusts from disuse; water loses its purity from stagnation...even so does inaction sap the vigor of the mind.

Leonardo da Vinci

Tell Your Face

One lunchtime, many years ago, I was in the supermarket in the local shopping mall around the corner from our practice. It wasn't busy, so only one checkout position was open, and there were five people in the line ahead of me. There was an elderly couple, who had half a dozen items, including a frozen chicken, then three other people with a few items each.

The checkout operator was a young lady who obviously wanted to be somewhere else that day, as she had a dreadful scowl on her face and was almost throwing the items down the counter after she had punched them into the register. She sent the frozen chicken down so fast that it bounced off the end and landed on the floor. The elderly gentleman said, "Excuse me, Miss. Do you mind if I replace that chicken? It will be dirty now it's been on the floor." "All right," she scowled. Excusing myself as I moved from the back of the line past the people ahead of me, I went to the front of the line, took out an "Expect a Miracle" card and placed it on the cash register, right in front of her face.

"Pardon me young lady, are you happy?" I said. "Yes," she scowled. "Well," I said, "please tell your face!" At that, everyone started to giggle, and eventually the laughter became so loud that it caught the attention of the store manager and assistant manager, who were standing next to the front window behind the registers, facing the store and discussing the day's business. They also burst into laughter, and then the young lady on the checkout started to laugh. "That's better," I said. "Your face knows you're happy now."

Tell Your Face

I returned to my position in the queue, and the people in the line ahead of me proceeded to complete their transactions and leave the store, one by one. When I eventually emerged, I found five people, none of whom knew each other prior to going into the store, standing around talking as if they had been friends for years. They stopped me and said, "Can you come over here, please? Do you have anymore of those cards?" "Sure," I said. "Can we all have one?" "Of course," I said, and proceeded to give them all a card.

In response to their questions, I told them I was a chiropractor just around the corner. Two of them said, "Can we come and see you as patients?" "Not a problem," I replied. Interestingly, by the end of the following week, four out of the five people I met that day had become patients. I hadn't gone out to solicit patients. I had just gone out to buy some things I needed, and had encountered a young lady who was exhibiting behavior that wasn't helping anybody. An "Expect a Miracle" card had transformed her attitude, and that of everybody in the vicinity. As a result, I met some wonderful people who became lifelong friends in my practice.

Dr. John Hinwood

Most people are about as happy as they make up their minds to be.

Abraham Lincoln

11

MIRACLES
OF SPORT

*Ingenuity + Courage and
Hard Work = Miracles*

Bob Richards

A Fishy Story

Ben had been a patient of mine for two months, so when he told me he was going away for a week on a fishing trip, I pulled out an "Expect a Miracle" card and handed it to him. "What am I supposed to do with this?" he said. "Take it with you on your fishing trip, and amazing things will happen," I replied.

He looked at me with a blank expression on his face and said, "What am I meant to do, take it out of my wallet and just dangle it in the water and the fish are going to jump into the boat?" "You can do whatever you want," I said. "If you think that will help, you can do that, but I would suggest just keeping it on you at all times, in your wallet most likely."

One week later, Ben walked in with a huge smile on his face and gave me a big 'thumbs up.' "Wow, that card really works!" he said. I laughed, and asked him what had happened. "What happened?" he replied. "In thirty years of fishing, I've never caught more crabs or more fish in one week!" He told me he had caught 200 male keeper mud crabs (he only kept 20, and threw the rest back) and all sorts of fish were almost literally jumping into his boat all week. He'd never experienced a fishing trip like it in his life, and was stunned by the power of the "Expect a Miracle" card. We were both blown away, and enjoyed a good laugh about it.

Dr. Clinton McCauley

There is Always a Silver Lining!

This story is important for a number of reasons. The event that it describes became a defining moment in my life, but more importantly, it became the cornerstone in my passion for helping people succeed in their lives. My hope is that it will provide you with the inspiration to find your true passion in life – whatever that might be. I love to see people excel, and much of that desire comes from years of playing team sports.

This is a story about a selfish young man, a severed Achilles tendon and a whole bunch of shattered dreams. Have you ever experienced a traumatic event in your life, only to find that the cloud that has descended over your life has a silver lining?

My first big decision in life was where to go to play college football. I was very fortunate in that I chose to play for the University of Iowa, whose head coach, Hayden Fry, was a great coach, and a great mentor. As a sophomore, I was starting kicker, breaking records, and destined to play professionally after college; life was great! Our game that weekend was due to be broadcast on national TV, and the point spread was two, so the pressure was on. I was looking for some advice, so I talked to a buddy of mine on the golf team. "Steve," I said, "the pressure is getting to me a little bit. I've got to get away for a few hours; let's go play a little golf."

"It was raining this morning," he said. "That's the pivotal word," I said "'*was*.' It's not raining now. Let's go play."

We were coming off the 12th green, which was elevated above the 13th tee box, and as we came over the top of the hill, the golf cart started going too fast. I tapped the brakes to slow us down, but the brakes locked and the cart spun sideways and started sliding faster and faster down the hill. We were coming down the hill faster sideways than you'd ever want to be going even facing the right direction. When we reached the bottom of the hill, the cart hit a mound and stopped, but I didn't. I was thrown out of the cart, which ran over my right foot, which was my kicking foot, completely severing my Achilles tendon.

All that time, all that effort, that professional future, all gone. I dug my toe in the ground so it wouldn't move, put my face in my hands and said, "Steve, call an ambulance. I'm going to need surgery this afternoon. I'm out for the season." The team doctor met us at the hospital and said "Scott, you're never going to play football again, in fact you're never going to play any sport again. You're going to be extremely lucky if you can even walk without a limp." "Sew me up, doc. I'll be back," I said.

As it turned out, he did a great job, because I did come back to play again, but that's not the unique part of this story. About halfway through the week that I spent in hospital recovering from the surgery, I noticed something unusual. All those friends, all those team mates, all the people who should have been coming to see me, hadn't come. It caused me to look at myself, and at what I had become. It allowed me to reflect on my dad's years of service speaking on behalf of United Way, driving people to charitable causes and helping other people, and it was then that I knew I needed to get back to who I was truly raised to be. Following that incident, and as a result of the desire for change that it produced within me, I went out into corporate America after I graduated and started training people. "It's not where you are in your life that counts, it's where you want to be. You can be anything you want to be," I would tell them, and as they started to experience success, I too felt successful. It was awesome being part of helping people achieve their dreams. But then, my company started messing me around.

Fortunately, my good friend Dr. Fabrizio Mancini came to me and said, "Scott, why don't you share the message of wellness through chiropractic care?" "Well, thanks, Fab, but I've got a job," I said. "I'm getting messed around, but I've got a job." Right then, he was offering me an opportunity that would change my life, but I didn't realize it. A couple of months later, he contacted me again and said, "How about now?" "That's it, I'm out of here," I said. I knew I didn't have the education necessary to go out and do what I was about to do, so I found the program that gave me that education. It cost $25,000, and I paid for it with my credit card before I had even discussed it with my wife. I knew she'd support me – I'll tell you about that shortly.

To cut a long story short, I completed that education process and then went on the road, where I met my first mentor, Jack Canfield. He took me aside one morning and said, "Scott, we all have far more talent and capabilities than we use in our day to day lives. In fact, we've only been put on this earth for two reasons, number one to have a fabulous life, and number two to help as many other people as we possibly can." It took me right back to the hospital room so many years ago when he continued, "If you're not having a fabulous life, chances are you're not helping anybody else. And if you're not having a fabulous life and you're not helping anybody else, you're robbing humanity, you're cheating humanity, in fact you're being selfish!" With that, he walked away.

That's a pretty heavy trip to lay on a guy. I went up to my room and thought about it for a long time before I eventually fell asleep. When I woke up the next morning, the proclamation that I've started virtually every day with ever since was ringing in my head. I don't know where it came from – it was just there. That proclamation is:

"I am attracting into my life everything that I need to cause over 100 million dollars in charitable giving!"

All of a sudden, I had this huge *what* that I wanted to accomplish in my life. I had no clue how that was going to happen, but the neat thing is, if you develop a big enough *what,* with a strong enough *why,* the *how* starts to show up soon enough!

I was talking to another mentor the next day, and I said, "John, you are so good. I want to be like you." "You want to be like me?" he said. "Yes sir, I certainly do." "Well, if you want to be like me, do what I do," he said. "That's it?" I said. "It's that easy? If I want to be like you, I just have to do what you do?" "Yeah," he said. "Are you serving as many people as you possibly can?" "Sure!" I said. "Are you really?" "Well, I guess I could do more," I replied sheepishly. He then suggested that I needed to really go inside my heart to gain a greater sense of what I could be doing. After a period of study and reflection, I went back to him and said, "John, I did it, I took control. I've taken complete ownership of my morning proclamation!" "Man, that's awesome," he said, "because formal education will make you a living, but self-education will give you true fulfillment."

Have you ever read the book *Think and Grow Rich* by Napoleon Hill? In the early 1900s, Hill interviewed the top 500 industrialists, the most wealthy people of his time, and he made two unique discoveries; first, they all shared 13 key characteristics. Now that in itself was exciting, but the second finding was far more important. None of them had been born with those key characteristics; they were all learned attributes. Why is this so important for us? Because if they were able to learn them, we can learn them too, and that's why I suggest you read *Think and Grow Rich*.

I'm not going to talk about the book any more, but let me give you the three success principles that have been pivotal in getting me to where I am today. The first is that you have to develop specialized knowledge in order to be successful in the area that you choose. You have to learn as much about that area of expertise as you possibly can. To be able to cause and generate over $100 million in charitable giving, I have consistently sought out the people and programs that have been successful in raising money and helping other people. Knowledge equals money, money that can be used to help so many worthy causes worldwide.

The second is that you then have to surround yourself with a mastermind team. When two minds come together, a third and greater mastermind is created. We are all a product of our experiences. You've had experiences, and I've had experiences, but when we come together, it's not one plus one equals two, it's really three, four or five; there's synergy there, because we can borrow from each other's experiences.

The third principle of success is that you have to be decisive in nature; you have to make decisions easily.

After seeking out the specialized knowledge that was necessary, we created a series of books, seminars, media productions, training systems, and websites – an all-encompassing campaign to fulfill the vision of causing over 100 million dollars in charitable giving. The first book, *Talking With Giants! Powerful Leaders Share Life Lessons*, supports 21 separate charities alone. The fifteen 'giants' who were interviewed for the book were mentors and friends, and they have since become part of the mastermind team working towards this common goal. The decision that had to be made was simple; get into action and move this project forward – gain traction. You can learn more by going to www.talkingwithgiants.com. It's amazing that when you simply come up with a big enough *what* and a strong enough *why,* the *hows* show up soon enough!

Now, you may be wondering what the outcome was of putting $25,000 on my credit card before discussing it with my wife. When it did come time to talk to her about it, I said, "Peggy, I made the decision to get the education necessary to move my dream of creating over 100 million dollars in charitable giving forward, and that education costs $25,000, and I've put it on my credit card." "Reeeeaaaallllly?" she said. "Scott, it's one of two things; either you're totally committed to making that decision work, or you need to be committed because you're nuts, and I've lived with you long enough to know that's not the case, so I'm behind you 100 percent!" That was the entire conversation. She's a sweet girl, and I'm a very blessed man. The sidebar to the story is that six and a half weeks after I finished the education course, I made the money to pay off the $25,000 on my credit card in just two days!

I've done that many times since, but would I have been able to do it even once without the education? Not a chance. Did I have to step outside my comfort zone? You bet. You see, I truly believe what my mentors have taught me. We have been put on this earth to have a fabulous life and to help as many people as we possibly can, and as a student of philanthropy, I experience the success and gratitude that comes from helping others virtually every day. The universe will deliver everything we need to fulfill our dreams, once we gain clarity on what it is that we want, and once we always expect a miracle to happen.

Because of that, I feel it's my responsibility to share it with you for your consideration. Now, do I think that learning to come from a servant heart and doing more for others is right for you? Yeah, I really do, but you know what; it doesn't matter what I think. It's not my decision; it's your decision.

However, there is another reason why I truly believe this story has been put before you today, and that's to encourage you. Just as I've got this huge *what* and *why* I want to accomplish in my life, you have huge *whats* and *whys* as well. It could be sending your kids or grandkids off to college, building a playground at a local school, adding a wing onto your church, but here's the one thing we all share in common; if we're not in control of our dreams and visions, do those things happen? No, so again, I truly believe I've been put here to encourage you. If philanthropy is the silver lining to your cloud, welcome to the *Talking With Giants!* family, but if it's not, find something that is. Don't let anybody steal your dreams. You've been put on this earth, just like me, to have a fabulous life and to help as many people as you possibly can, and when you live your life that way, it's just a blast; it's just plain fun!

You see, what happened to me on that golf cart that day so long ago was a blessing in disguise. I was headed in the wrong personal direction, and I got redirected into a bigger and better dream, that of helping other people. Writing the *Talking With Giants!* series of books and creating products designed to support philanthropic causes and this system has been the vehicle that's allowed me to help so many, and it can help you too, if you let it. Follow your hearts, follow your passions – your silver lining awaits! And always remember to expect a miracle.

Scott Schilling

Open Sesame

I had just got back from an Australian summer where the temperature often reached 40 °C and there were widespread water restrictions, and now things were somewhat different at my home on Lake Garda, Italy, where it was snowing! It doesn't snow on the lake all that often, but it sure is nice when it does. The wind was also good, and I was keen to get out kiteboarding so I could put my new dry suit to the test. The next day was going to be epic for snowboarding, but today, my kite needed to get some exercise.

I rigged up my gear, along with a couple of other guys who were ready to go out, and was glad to get my dry suit on, as my hands were feeling the cold. When you go out in extreme conditions, it pays to ride with others so you can keep an eye on each other in case something goes wrong. I launched the other kiters, and then hit the water myself. They say that in February the temperature of the water in the lake is about 8 °C, but all I can say is that it was way too cold to drink, and I planned to spend most of my time in the air or on my board. Alas, it was not to be! After riding for a while, I made a jump, but a wind gust pulled me out of shape and, from a height of about five meters, I hit the water at about the same time as my kite. Cold water makes for a solid impact, kind of like getting hit in the face by a wet soccer ball on a cold winter's day, only bigger. When your kite goes down, you need to grab one of the lines and reel in a couple of meters, and this is when I realized I could be in trouble. My hands were so cold, I had trouble feeling and gripping, and the line kept slipping. I kept trying for a minute or so, conscious of the icy water that was rapidly cooling my hands, feet and limbs, then stopped for a moment to calm myself and assess my predicament.

I was comforted by the fact that there were other kite-boarders and windsurfers out on the lake, until I looked around. When you are down at water level, you suddenly realize how far away everything is. I had drifted downwind, and was now on my own. The nearest shore was a good two-kilometer swim away – not good! I made several attempts to get my kite out of the water, to no avail. The wind seemed to have dropped off, and the kite wouldn't launch, and although my suit was keeping out the icy water, my body was steadily cooling down. I had to get to shore. I tried cursing and screaming, but that didn't work, so I tried swimming to get my kite into a launch position, but that just pulled me further away from shore.

I was now even further away from the other people out on the lake, and realized that I had no choice but to rescue myself. I unhooked my kite bar, pulled the kite toward me and slightly deflated the kite so that I could hold both lateral edges to form a C-shape in the hope that it would capture sufficient wind to drag me to safety. Leaning the kite towards the nearest shore, I began 'body dragging,' kicking my legs as I went to keep the blood circulating. Downwind of me, the lake stretched to the horizon, and at the angle at which I was headed towards the shore, it was clear that I would be dragging for some time before I eventually reached dry land. The mountains looked so beautiful from the middle of the lake, and the snow that was falling into the valley made the scene truly wild. I remember thinking, "This boy is a long way from Oz now."

It took a lot of energy to hold the kite toward the shore, as each gust of wind seemed to pull it in the opposite direction. At times, the wind dropped right off, leaving me bobbing in the water, and although I hadn't yet started to cramp, my legs were definitely tightening up. I simply had to get to shore, sooner rather than later. I had been dragging for some time, and the shore was getting steadily closer, when I started to worry about my suit springing a leak. If I'd been in my usual wetsuit, I would have been a frozen popsicle by now. I was now approaching the shore, and even though I was successfully resisting the cold, my problems were not yet over. As I surveyed the shoreline, I could see that I was approaching the town of Malcesine. The nearest building was a castle built on top of a cliff face that fell directly into the water. No chance of landing there. After that was the town, which had no beaches, just walls and buildings. Where was I supposed to land? Water had started to seep into my suit, making my movements heavy and cumbersome. My legs were starting to cramp up, and my hands and feet were frozen, and were burning like crazy. I needed to warm up, and soon.

Suddenly, I noticed that there was a door set into the wall next to the castle, just above the surface of the water. I needed someone to open the door. Lo and behold, what did I see? A little old lady was peering over the wall and frantically waving me over. I couldn't believe my eyes. There was no-one around at all, except for this one angel at the place where it looked like I was going to be pummelled against the wall. I could feel myself losing strength as I made my way slowly towards the door. The next thing I saw was the door in the wall opening, and the elderly lady beckoning me toward her. I was saved! However, as I approached the open door, I noticed that just below the surface of the crashing waves were the rusty remains of an old pier. Dangerous! I had my inflatable kite and around 120 meters of line to maneuver through the tangled mess of rusted iron before I could reach the door. I deflated my kite, made spaghetti of my lines, and my angel helped to pull me out of the water. I staggered through the doorway, and was astounded to see my new surroundings. I was now in a beautiful private garden that was a riot of color.

My savior turned out to be as caring toward me as my own grandmother. She offered me shelter until I warmed up, and a change of clothes. I politely declined, as I needed to pack my gear and get back to my car. I was cold, and wanted to keep moving, as I had a long walk ahead of me, but she wasn't having it, so for the next hour or so we sat by the fire and drank hot tea and ate biscuits. She introduced me to her caretakers, who helped me to sort out all my gear. There I was, warming myself with tea and bikkies beneath the towers of a castle in this beautifully manicured Garden of Eden on the edge of a lake while outside it was snowing. I knew it had been a miracle that I hadn't perished, but here I was in heaven, all the same. What a day!

Dr. Mario Stefano

The glad hand is all right in sunshine, but it's the helping hand on a dark day that folks remember to the end of time.

Amadeo Peter Giannini

12

MIRACLES OF TRAVEL

A person needs at intervals to separate from family and companions and go to new places. One must go without familiars in order to be open to influences, to change.

Katharine Butler Hathaway

You're Joking, Aren't You?

Two days before my wife, my son and I were due to fly back to Australia after our four-week holiday in South Africa, I realized that the return plane trip that was booked was not what we had intended. The plane would fly from Johannesburg to Melbourne, but there would be a stopover in Perth on the way, and we wouldn't arrive in Melbourne until midnight, and I was supposed to be starting work early the next morning. This was on our itinerary, but I had totally overlooked it. I called Qantas and discussed the possibility of changing to the South African Airways (SAA) flight that was departing on the same day. After spending an hour on the phone, I learned that this would be extremely expensive after paying cancellation and rebooking fees together with additional airport taxes, so I decided to leave things as they stood.

The day we were leaving, my mom called the airline thirty minutes before we were scheduled to leave to drive to Johannesburg International Airport to check that the flight was on time and was told that it would be leaving 18 hours later than scheduled. It was now late Saturday afternoon, we had packed our bags ready to leave, had a six-month-old baby who was starting to whinge due to lack of attention and I had patients booked in to see me on the Monday morning. Knowing that there was an SAA flight bound for Australia within 10 minutes of the Qantas flight we were supposed to be on, we decided to take our chances and drive to the airport. I called SAA on the way, and they told me that the flight was full, except for two seats in business class.

We arrived at the airport, which was as busy as ever. There were long queues for check-in for the SAA flight, and from what we could see, many frustrated Qantas customers due to the delay in the flight we were meant to be on. I decided to rush to the ticket sales counter, where there was a queue of about 15 people and just two staff serving. As they say, TIA (This Is Africa). While we waited in the line, we began chatting with a number of other people, some of whom had the same problem as us. A man three positions ahead of us in the line was called up, but after five minutes of talking with the ticket assistant, he left the counter after being told that the only way he could get onto the SAA flight was by paying almost $9,000 to upgrade his existing Qantas ticket to business class on SAA. He had decided to wait the 18 hours.

It was another 45 minutes before we eventually reached the counter, and that was only because they had opened a third position. A lovely African lady asked how she could help me. "My wife and I and our six-month-old baby were booked on the Qantas flight, but it's been delayed," I said. "I know that it's impossible to transfer from the Qantas flight to the SAA flight this evening but..." Then I handed her an "Expect a Miracle" card. She smiled, and then laughed, almost as if to say 'You're joking, aren't you?' Then she asked for our tickets, and left the counter. My wife joined me at the counter to find out what was happening. When she looked down at the desk and saw the "Expect a Miracle" card, she said, "Don't tell me you're still giving those cards out!"

Thirty minutes later, the lady returned and gave us two pieces of paper which signified a no-charge transfer onto the desired SAA flight and the connecting Qantas flight from Perth to Melbourne. We were ushered to the first class check-in counters, and were seated three rows from the front with a spare seat for our baby on the trip from Johannesburg, and in the front row in economy with a baby bassinet on the flight from Perth to Melbourne. Our bags were tagged with priority stickers so they would be the first ones out when we reached Perth, and we were checked in at the first class counter in Perth, while there was a queue an hour long for economy check-in.

After what was initially a stressful time, we arrived home safely and earlier than we would have even if the original flight hadn't been delayed. So, when in doubt, remember…expect a miracle!

Dr. Roy Smith

It is no use saying, 'We are doing our best.' You have got to succeed in doing what is necessary.

Winston Churchill

Have I Got a
Deal For You!

A few years ago, I was in New York and had to travel to New Jersey to speak the next day. If you've ever been at JFK Airport around 5 p.m. on a weekday, you'll know it's like being in a human zoo. I wasn't sure what I needed to do to continue on to New Jersey, so I went down to Ground Transportation in search of assistance.

When I got there, I saw people lined up two and three deep at the counter, and many were yelling out demanding attention. It was incredibly noisy and there were only three service agents behind the counter, all very motherly African American women.

Eventually I managed to edge forward until I was within reach of the counter. I pulled out an "Expect a Miracle" card and extended my arm. One of the women saw the card and grabbed it from my hand. She read it and yelled, "Brother, are you born again?" "Well, I tell you, I always expect a miracle," I replied. She then asked me where I wanted to go. I told her I needed to get to Teaneck, New Jersey. "Teaneck, New Jersey?" she said. Well, that's going to take about an hour and a half." "Wow, that's excellent, I replied. "How do I get there? What are the modes of transport?" "Well, you can take the bus for $77, or you can take the shuttle, or you can take a taxi cab, or you can take a Town Car," she said. "Yes, that would be great," I said. "What else is there?" "Well, you can take a limo, and then there's the super limo," she said, "and all those just go up in price, sir. They go right up in price." Great, I thought.

She looked at my card again and said, "Man, this is a special card." Then she showed it to her colleagues. "Can we all have one of those cards, sir?" "Absolutely," I said. I gave them all a card and they examined them and discussed them while people continued to yell out their demands. Then the lady who had taken the first card disappeared into a back room. She soon returned and said, "Have I got a deal for you, sir!" "What's that, Ma'am?" I said. "Well sir, I got you a super limo for $77, the same price as the bus." "Thank you, Ma'am," I said. "That's wonderful."

I walked outside and saw two fellows who had boarded the plane with me in Brisbane and had also flown the entire Brisbane/Sydney/Los Angeles/New York trip, a 29-hour journey, standing in the long bus queue. I crossed the road just in time to see a shiny grey super limo slide around the corner. Man, it was a big sucker! You could have fitted an entire football team inside! It had two TVs and two bars, and I almost needed a megaphone to speak to the driver. It was an absolutely superb hour and a half drive down to Teaneck, New Jersey, all thanks to that little card. Those ladies at Ground Transportation were so happy and excited to receive the card. It made their day in among the chaos, and for me it was a miracle ending to a long journey.

Dr. John Hinwood

He that can have patience can have what he will.

Benjamin Franklin

The Magical
Mystery Tour

In November 2007, I was heading out to Phuket, Thailand
to crew on the yacht Millennium in Asia's biggest sail-
ing regatta, The King's Cup. I had also crewed on the
boat the previous year when we won line honors in the Dent
Island to Dunk Island Classic along Australia's Great Bar-
rier Reef. It had been a special experience, and I was ex-
cited to be going to Thailand and crewing on Millennium
once again.

My flight was scheduled to leave at midnight, so my wife
Judy drove me to Brisbane Airport, an hour and a half jour-
ney, and I joined the check-in queue at 10 p.m., but it was
slow going progressing toward the counter. As 11 p.m. ap-
proached, the conveyor belts behind the check-in counter
suddenly stopped, and about 15 minutes later a Thai Airways
representative walked along the line telling us that the plane
that had been scheduled to take us to Bangkok had broken
down in Sydney, and would not be arriving in Brisbane for
another 24 hours.

Three other flights with other airlines were all leaving
around midnight for Bangkok, however they were all booked
out. The airline sent all the passengers who lived in or near
Brisbane home for the night, and then set about trying to find
hotel rooms for the 94 remaining passengers, but discovered
that, at this hour of night, there were only three hotel rooms
available, which they allocated to the three disabled persons
booked on our flight.

The airline arranged for one of the airport's coffee shops to remain open to feed and water the rest of us while they extended their search for accommodation to the Gold and Sunshine Coasts, popular holiday destinations one hour south and north of Brisbane respectively. At 1.30 a.m., a greatly relieved Thai Airways representative came to the coffee shop to inform us that he had secured 90 rooms at the Surfers Paradise Holiday Inn on the Gold Coast, and we would all be taken there by individual taxi cabs.

We collected our bags and joined the queue for cabs outside. I was travelling with two friends, Craig Gilberd and his partner Karen Cooke, both of whom have extensive sailing experience, and we shared a cab. Our Ethiopian cab driver was a fun-filled man who informed us as we were driving out of the airport that as it was now nearly 2 a.m. and our cab ride to the hotel was over an hour each way, he would need to go and find his 'day driver' to take us to Surfers Paradise.

After a half-hour 'magical mystery tour' around Brisbane, we finally found his relieving driver, who set off to drive us to Surfers Paradise, however there was one small problem. It was a typically warm, sub-tropical night in south-east Queensland and the cab's air conditioning was broken. It was clear that our new driver had an aversion to soap and water, and the cab was decidedly 'on the nose.' The odor in that cab took me back to my days spent backpacking around Asia and Latin America in the early 1970s.

By 3.30 a.m., I was snug in bed on the 19th floor of the Holiday Inn at Surfers Paradise, and the clean white sheets and fresh sea air made a pleasant change indeed. I woke at 9 a.m. to be greeted by a beautiful, sunny day and fantastic views of the beach and the Pacific Ocean. A note from the airline had been slipped under my door while I slept which said I should have breakfast and lunch on the airline, check out by 12 noon and be ready to be bussed back to Brisbane at 2 p.m.

Before I boarded the bus that had arrived to take us back to Brisbane, I telephoned my travel agent of over 20 years and asked her to check to see when our plane would be repaired. She reported that it looked like two or three days, as they still hadn't been able to secure the part that was needed. On arriving back at Brisbane International Airport, we joined the extremely long queue to check in once again. As the line was so long, a Thai Airways representative gave us each a meal voucher and suggested we go to the food court and relax for a while before returning to check in later in the afternoon.

As we had time to kill, and my wife Judy had asked me to buy her an iPod, I decided to go shopping at the Duty Free shop with Craig. Some thirty minutes later we returned to join Karen, who had been relaxing and reading a book over a cup of coffee. Karen was excited, because an elderly woman she had met on the bus journey back from the Gold Coast hotel had just told her that the Thai Airways booking agent had offered to fly her across Australia from Brisbane to Perth, a flight similar in length to that from New York to Los Angeles. The airline would overnight her in a Perth hotel, then fly her to Phuket at 10 a.m. the next morning.

The woman had told Karen that she had declined this offer, because "everybody knows that to fly to Phuket, first you first have to fly to Bangkok and then change planes." Instead, the lady was going to have a coffee and a sandwich before heading home to wait until the plane was repaired. My travel agent had told me earlier in the day that, as we were flying high season, all the airlines flying out of Brisbane to South-east Asian destinations were booked out, but that maybe they would be able to re-route us via New Zealand or another Australian capital city to get us to Phuket in time to join our boat.

The three of us looked at each other and then headed straight back to the check-in counter.

The couple ahead of us in the line were Indians on their way to Bangkok and then on to Mumbai where the lady was to be Matron of Honor at a big wedding, and if they didn't arrive in Bangkok by early the next morning they wouldn't reach Mumbai in time for the wedding. They were not happy campers, and were very rude, really giving the check-in agent a rough time. Eventually, the agent asked them to move to one side and discuss a couple of alternatives he had suggested, saying that he would be with them shortly.

It's always wonderful to be next in line after people like that, because it gives you the opportunity to move the pendulum from the extremely negative and abusive area to the positive, warm, loving, expectant end of the scale. The person who has been on the receiving end of the previous customer's wrath immediately warms to you, and goes out of their way to see that you leave with a positive outcome.

I assumed the role of check-in person for Craig, Karen and myself, and as I stepped up to the counter, I extended my right hand to shake hands with the agent. This surprised him, however he already seemed much happier as he stood up and responded. I then placed three "Expect a Miracle" cards on the counter, one for the agent and one for each of his two female assistants, who were busy making phone calls to other airlines, writing out paper transfer tickets and attending to the many other tasks that were required.

"Ah, Phuket," said the agent. "This is a very difficult task tonight. The earliest I can get you there is tomorrow night." I then asked him about flying from Brisbane to Perth courtesy of Thai Airways and then catching the direct flight to Phuket at 10 a.m. the next morning. After several phone calls and many clicks of his mouse, the agent said, "Yes, there are six seats left on the Phuket flight. I have reserved three for you, however the 7.30 p.m. flight from Brisbane to Perth is full, so there is no way for you to connect with the flight to Phuket tomorrow morning. I just can't get you to Perth in time."

I then told the agent that my trusty "Expect a Miracle" cards always worked, and asked him if one of his assistants could please call Qantas at the domestic terminal and wait on the line until three cancellations showed up. It was now 6.40 p.m. and the flight was due to leave in forty minutes. The agent called his two assistants over, gave each of them an "Expect a Miracle" card and asked them if they were prepared to give it a go. All of a sudden they became excited and said "Let's do it!" with an air of positive expectation. One of the women worked the telephone to Qantas, while the three of us continually smiled at her. Ten minutes passed, then bingo! The woman's face was a picture of total excitement as she yelled out, "I got them, I got them, you have three seats to Perth, three people have just cancelled!"

Within five minutes they had written out the transfer ticket for the three of us, and told us that they would leave a message on my mobile phone to tell us which hotel they had booked us into when we arrived in Perth around midnight. We raced out of the International Terminal, grabbed a cab, and reached the Domestic Terminal just in time to check in before boarding commenced.

Our Perth detour was an unexpected surprise, and all three of us took advantage of our unscheduled visit. Two of Karen's four adult children live there, as do Craig's sister and family, including a special niece who had only returned to Australia from Egypt a few days earlier prior to giving birth to her first child, and I was able to catch up with our senior mentor for our Centre for Powerful Practices. Wow...thanks to Thai Airways, we enjoyed a celebration breakfast with our special group prior to flying to Thailand. We eventually arrived in Phuket a day behind schedule, but right on time for the King's Cup Regatta. Thanks to the "Expect a Miracle" card, we had enjoyed a truly magical mystery tour.

Dr. John Hinwood

Imagination is more important than knowledge. Knowledge is limited. Imagination encircles the world.

Albert Einstein

13

MIRACLES OF WORK

The heights by great men reached and kept/Were not attained by sudden flight/But they, while their companions slept/Were toiling upward in the night.

Henry Wadsworth Longfellow

Get Me to the Circus on Time

It was nearly 7 p.m. on a Saturday night when we walked out the front door of the Las Vegas Hilton Hotel to find to our astonishment that the cab queue was over 500 people long. We were speaking at the Parker Seminar, which is a huge annual worldwide meeting of chiropractors and chiropractic assistants, and the day's sessions had ended at 6.30 p.m. We hadn't realized that so many seminar attendees were staying in other hotels in Vegas and needed cabs, in addition to the normal cab traffic that the Las Vegas Hilton generates all day every day.

Some Canadian friends had discovered at the last minute that they were unable to attend the seminar, and had given us their tickets to the special Cirque du Soleil water show 'O', which was the talk of Las Vegas at the time. Our immediate thought was, "Oh no, how can we possibly get to the theatre on time; we'll miss the start of the show, and not be allowed in until the interval."

That morning, my wife Judy and I had met with a group of Japanese chiropractors who were at the seminar with a view to taking the Parker Seminar to Japan the following year. The President of the Parker Seminar, Dr. Fabrizio Mancini, had asked us to outline to them how we had sponsored the Parker Seminar in Melbourne, Australia, the previous year. The Japanese group were extremely grateful for the time we spent answering their questions, and for the advice we were able to give them, and our "Expect a Miracle" cards

141

were happily received.

Now, our twenty new friends from Japan were near the front of the cab line. As soon as they saw us step out of the front door of the hotel, we were greeted with, "Oh, Mr Dr. John, Mrs Dr. Judy – photo please?" The photo shoot was on, and while we were posing for numerous photographs, I took the opportunity to ask their interpreter if it was possible for us to join their group and take the first available cab, as we needed to get to a very special show in town urgently.

"Oh yes, Mr Dr. John, you need to expect a miracle," she replied, producing the card I had given her earlier that day, and said they would be only too happy for us to join them at the head of the queue. We arrived at the theatre just as the doors were closing and took our seats for an amazing show that was definitely a miracle event.

Dr. John Hinwood

Start by doing what's necessary, then what's possible, and suddenly you are doing the impossible.

St Francis of Assisi

They're Not All Butchers

Apart of my vocation involves visiting fellow chiropractors around the world to review their practices over several areas, ranging from clinical best practice to business management, communication and practice development. I had flown to Sydney to conduct one of these practice reviews, and as I got into the cab at the airport and gave the driver my client's address, I also gave her an "Expect a Miracle" card, as is my custom, which she received graciously.

As we drove towards the doctor's office, I told the driver that the place I was going to was a chiropractic centre, which would probably make it easier to find when we arrived at the street in question. Up until then, the cab driver had been really chatty, but as soon as I said the words 'chiropractic centre' there was stony cold silence in the cab. After about five minutes of this clearly uncharacteristic silence, my cabbie finally blurted out in an angry, emphatic voice, "Chiropractors are butchers!"

I remained silent for a minute or so and then replied, "You're right, some chiropractors are butchers, like some cab drivers are butchers, some motor mechanics are butchers, some lawyers are butchers, some hairdressers are butchers, and some dressmakers are butchers. Every vocation in life has its butchers."

"Why do you say chiropractors are butchers?" I asked. She proceeded to tell me that two days earlier she had taken her elderly mother to a chiropractor and he had hurt her badly, and now she couldn't move her neck, and was in great pain.

They're Not All Butchers

She told me that she would never take her mother to a chiropractor again, as they were now all butchers in her mind. "Unfortunately, our profession does have a very small number of butchers," I said, "and I imagine you know a few cab drivers who are also butchers, and you would never let your mom get into their cabs." She agreed that this was true. "Have you ever had a hairdresser butcher your hair?" I asked. "Oh yes," she said. "It was horrible!"

We then started to talk about the things that happen in life, and I told my cabbie that the woman chiropractor I was about to visit was a kind and gentle soul who cared for a diverse group of patients, from burly truck drivers to tiny new-born babies. Maybe her mother could visit the doctor whose rooms we were about to arrive at, I said, as I could give her and her mother a 100% guarantee that this wonderful chiropractor would not hurt her mother, in fact she could assist her mother to heal.

All of a sudden, my driver relaxed and started to become excited at the thought that there was another side to things, and maybe with the right chiropractor her mother could be helped. It was then that I reminded my driver to look again at the little card I had given her on getting into the cab. "Oh yes," she said. "I do expect a miracle now. Thank you." Her mother lived on the other side of Sydney and didn't drive, so the cabbie asked me if I knew of another excellent chiropractor in her mother's area.

As it happened I did know a particular doctor close to her mother, and after calling my office for his number, I phoned him, explained the situation and had him speak briefly with the cabbie. I then made an appointment for her mother with his assistant. I assured the cabbie that this chiropractor was a gifted, caring and truly amazing man.

We finally arrived at my client's office, and when we pulled up, my cab driver leapt out of the car, raced around to

144

open my door, and then gave me a big hug, shed a tear, and thanked me for what I had done for her mother. She told me that from now on, she would always expect a miracle, and she'd treasure the little card I had given her.

Dr. John Hinwood

> *The supreme quality for leadership is unquestionably integrity. Without it no real success is possible, no matter whether it's on a football field, in an army or in an office.*
>
> *Dwight Eisenhower*

14

MIRACLES
OF THE AGES

*And in the end, it's not the
years in your life that count.
It's the life in your years.*

Abraham Lincoln

An Old and Very Precious Card

There was a chiropractor at a seminar I was facilitating a number of years ago who told me that he had an elderly 89-year-old woman on a walker come in to see him. It took a very long time to process this lady because of her disabilities. This doctor ran a huge practice in a rural area of Australia, and he said that subsequent visits were going to be very difficult for him because of the huge amount of time this lady took, so he decided that, as the aged care home she was living in was quite near to his home, in future he would do house calls.

On his first visit there, he entered her room and noticed an "Expect a Miracle" card in a small frame above the bed, just like the ones he had seen me handing out for years.

"Where did you get that card?" he said. "Oh, I got that many years ago from my chiropractor who I used to see at Underwood near Brisbane before I had to move up here to come into the home." This was many years later, and yet she still had that card in a little frame above her bed in the nursing home. "I look at that card every day", she said. I know that me still being alive today is a miracle, and I just love that little card."

Those cards have brought huge joy to many, many people, and that is such a gift for me.

Dr. John Hinwood

You Don't Bring
Me Flowers

Early in 2006, we moved across the border from our 10-acre property on top of a mountain in a very beautiful rural area to our new home/office in a beach house in another State. On Saturday morning, the day after our move, our two personal assistants came in to the office in their own time to make sure they were settled into the new space, ready for a busy upcoming week.

Late in the afternoon, my wife Judy and I went for a drive and found a great florist in a mall only fifteen minutes from our new office. We purchased two massive sheaths of beautiful flowers to say thank you for the extra effort our amazing personal assistants had put in. As we arrived back at our car prior to leaving the mall, a sprightly woman, who appeared to be in her mid-eighties, alighted from the car next to us.

She was immediately transfixed by the bunches of flowers. "Oh, they are the most beautiful flowers I have ever seen," she said. "There are two very fortunate ladies who will be receiving them." My wife Judy and I replied together, "Absolutely!" This dear woman, still overawed by the beauty of the flowers, then said, "I wish that sometime in my life I could receive a sheath of flowers like those."

The only time most women ever receive flowers like these is either when they marry, or at their funeral, when they are no longer around to enjoy them. Judy and I looked at each other, smiled, and then said to this sweet woman, "We would like you to have one of these bunches of flowers as a gift from us to you, because you are so wonderful." I also gave her an "Expect a Miracle" card. "Oh, no I didn't mean that," she said. "I didn't want you to give me one of the sheaths of flowers. They must be so expensive. I can't accept them." We finally managed to persuade this elderly lady who, we discovered, was a widow that she really did deserve the flowers, and after her emotions and tears had settled, we drove off in different directions.

Several weeks later, Judy was doing our grocery shopping in a supermarket at the same mall when she saw an elderly woman struggling to reach some coffee that was on a high shelf. "Can I help you?" said Judy. "Yes, please!" came the reply. As she spoke, the lady turned around, whereupon they recognized each other from our encounter in the car park several weeks earlier. Judy and the elderly lady gave each other a big hug. She then told Judy that it had truly been a miracle that she had received the flowers several weeks earlier. She said the flowers had lasted for three weeks, and had given her a totally different perspective towards strangers. Further, the "Expect a Miracle" card had added so much to her attitude about life, even at 86 years of age. The only sorry note that the woman shared with Judy was that, of all the residents in the aged care facility where she lived, only one had believed the story of the gift of the flowers and the "Expect a Miracle" card. None of the other residents could believe that someone could receive such a gift from total strangers.

Judy and I loved the experience, and felt truly gifted. It was also a miracle for us.

Dr. John Hinwood

A Boy's First Miracle

When I was 12 years old, I was invited to take a fishing trip with my father and some other men from our church. This was significant for me in at least three ways:

A special one-on-one time with my dad which most boys long for. As an only son, this was especially true for me.

An opportunity to fish on a beautiful lake in the spring, when the fish should be biting, and the prospect of being with men doing "men's stuff."

A camp for men and boys only in the wilderness of Oklahoma that included singing, preaching and much fellowship.

The fishing was fantastic, with increasingly successful days that lasted from before dawn until after dark. We would clean the day's catch and cook a few fish up fresh with eggs for a late dinner. And, on the last day, I caught more fish than my dad did!

We slept in a six-man tent, and the men that we shared our tent with teased me for years afterwards for talking in my sleep one night saying, "I can't make it to shore." My dad woke me up, because he knew I was a deep sleeper, and all I probably needed was to go to the toilet.

The miracle occurred at the men's camp we attended later that week. It was held in a very remote, rugged, poor socio-economic area of south-east Oklahoma, and there were approximately 5,000 men and boys in attendance. There was no running water, so no flushing toilets, and it was definitely a visual and olfactory experience to walk into my first "twenty-holer." This contrasted with the experience of hearing 5,000 male voices singing songs of praise in a large steel tent (a structure with a roof but no sides). I still get goose bumps thinking about it, even as I'm writing this!

The miracle of faith happened on the last night, when there was an appeal for offerings to support the local churches. We had visited one of these local churches, seemingly in the middle of nowhere, the previous evening, and had experienced the warm hospitality of these friendly people, but these churches had very little in the way of resources. As a city boy, I was shocked to see wild goat served, and so I understood that the need of these mountain churches was great.

In response to the announcement of the appeal, I resolved to give the rest of my pocket money, two dollars. Then, the preacher who was leading the appeal asked us to pray. He asked us to step out in faith, and double whatever amount we had decided to give. There I was, 12 years old, with no further resources, and therefore no possibility of doubling my offering. I couldn't see any way for my prayer to be answered, but I prayed for my offering to double anyway. While my eyes were still closed, my father tapped me on the shoulder and, without saying word, handed me a pack of nickels. When I opened my eyes and counted them, there was exactly two dollars!

Needless to say, I was amazed. To me, God heard a simple prayer from a young boy and answered it almost before the words could be uttered. Acting in faith would never be the same again.

Dr. Douglas L Herron

A Pathway to Experiencing Miracles

I am fortunate enough to have very frequent communication with John and Judy Hinwood, and of course with this comes copious quantities of these magic little "Expect a Miracle" cards.

A small confession here: I am a goal freak, consequently I know that having a simple, concise method of setting goals and following through to completion is a must for any form of success. I teach it, I live it and I breathe it. One essential key here is reading my/your top ten goals daily, even twice daily or more.

One morning while I was writing my goals, I glanced at my considerable stack of "Expect a Miracle" cards and a wonderful idea came to me – writing my goals on the back of these cards. Wow! An "Expect a Miracle/Goal" flip card. I used to use flip cards with huge success while studying, and now it is part of my goal-setting method.

I still write my daily goals in my diary, and now carry a stack of ten cards with me so I can flip through them at my convenience. Whenever I have an idle moment, I can flip through these little gems. They literally keep me on track, more than ever before.

So, what impact has this had on my life over the last six months? I now have much more order in my life, increased focus on my priorities and acceleration toward where I am going. Using these "Expect a Miracle" flip cards regularly throughout the day keeps these priorities foremost in my focus. The result? I'm able to move one step beyond "Expecting a Miracle" to "Experiencing a Miracle."

Thank you, John – please keep sending those "Expect a Miracle" cards to me!

Dr. Craig Gilberd

If you don't design your own life plan, chances are you'll fall into someone else's. And guess what they might have planned for you? Not much.

Jim Rohn

Thirteen Tips for Miracle-making Magic!

1. Think, talk and act positively in all circumstances. No matter what!

2. Ask yourself whenever you face a challenge, "What would be the best outcome in this situation?"

3. Find time to just sit and put your brain into freewheeling mode. Just let it run free…busy brains sometimes miss miracles!

4. Miracles don't necessarily come with a clap of thunder or a flash of lightning…sometimes they come on tippy-toe.

5. Go with the flow…sometimes at first sight the miracles we get don't appear to be the ones we want.

6. Miracles come when you least expect them…make them welcome whenever they arrive.

7. Help enough others get their miracles and it's amazing what a positive life you create.

8. Look for the miracles around you…a bird on the wing, the beauty of a rose, the smile of a child. When you see the miracles that already exist, new ones arrive.

9. It's okay to ask...miracles are for everyone, and we all deserve them.

10. Abundance abounds...there are plenty of miracles for us all.

11. When you are totally open to receiving miracles, it's astounding how they find their way to you and you become a 'miracle magnet.'

12. If you continually ASK for what you really want in life, the funny thing is, you will very often get it.

13. Print off some Expect A Miracle cards from our www.expect-a-miracle.net website and start handing them out. They'll work like boomerangs and come back to you as you continue to spread the miracle expectancy.

Share Your Miracle Stories

Share your miracle stories with the rest of the world. If you have a miracle story of your own (or someone else's) that you feel would enhance the lives of others, please post it on **www.expect-a-miracle.net**.

The best stories received each year will be included in future volumes of *You Can...Expect a Miracle!*

In addition, you could win free copies of the current volume of *You Can...Expect a Miracle!* if your story is voted the Readers' Choice Story of the Week. Weekly winners will be eligible to win a trip around the world for two people if their story is voted the Readers' Choice Story of the Year.

We will make sure that you (and the author, if you are not the author) are credited for your contribution. Thank you!

VISIT OUR WEBSITE

www.expect-a-miracle.net

If you know someone who has a heartfelt or dynamite story to tell, please pass this website address on to them and invite them to join us in energizing the mental and emotional health of people around the world.

If you register on the website, you will receive our Expect a Miracle Weekly Newsletter.

WIN A HOLIDAY FOR TWO AROUND THE WORLD

Simply submit your miracle story into the appropriate category on the website.

Each week our readers will choose a story of the week.

The Readers' Choice Story of the Week winners will each receive a copy of this volume of "You Can...Expect a Miracle" and become eligible for the holiday for two around the world, which will be awarded to the story voted **"Readers' Choice Story of the Year."**

Sources and Permissions

To protect the privacy of clients of the health-care practitioners who have contributed stories for this book, some of the names in the stories have been changed.

Every effort has been made to ensure that each author has been properly acknowledged.

The story 'The Shopkeeper' by Pat Hicks has previously been published elsewhere and is the property of:

iwantafreecreditreport.com,
Copyright © freshstartcreditscores.com.

'The Power That Made the Body Heals the Body' by Gilles Lemarche has been reprinted from Chiropractic Wellness and Fitness Magazine.

Looking for a Speaker for Your Next Conference, Seminar or Workshop?

You can contact Dr. John Hinwood at the address below for speaking engagements.

Dr. Scott Walker, the Founder of Neuro Emotional Technique from California, USA wrote this note after I spoke to his seminar group about 'Expecting Miracles' in November 2007:

"I was attending a NET SUCCESS Chiropractic Seminar in Northern New South Wales, Australia. Dr. John Hinwood was presenting to the group, and asked if there were any volunteers among this group of over 100 chiropractors who would be willing to share a miracle they had witnessed in their practice.

"As is typical in such a group, a few brave souls who were not afraid of speaking in public got up and shared some miracles they had seen. Fair enough so far. Most of the attendees said nothing, but applauded the doctors who did share. Then Dr. Hinwood asked the audience to write about any miracles they had witnessed.

"I was overwhelmed. Why? Without hesitation, every single one of the hundred attendees immediately put pen to paper to write about a miracle they had witnessed. There was no pondering or scratching of heads wondering how to phrase things, but an instant and ongoing flow of written descriptions. Apparently miracles were not hard to come by!

Imagine, one hundred people being able to recall a miracle they had witnessed at the drop of a hat. It appeared that each of them could have come up with several miracles. That so many people were instantly able to recount one miracle was and is miraculous in its own right."

Dr. John Hinwood
Expect a Miracle
PO Box 1607
Kingscliff NSW 2487
Australia
Phone: + 61 2 6674 0777
Fax: + 61 2 6674 0377
Email: johnh@expect-a-miracle.net
Website: www.expect-a-miracle.net

Ordering Additional Copies of this Book

If you would like to order additional copies of this book, either single copies or volume quantities for gift giving, please email us at info@expect-a-miracle.net or visit us at www.executivebooks.com or www.expect-a-miracle.net.

About the Author

Dr John Hinwood is an author, international speaker, mentor, coach and consultant whose clients are 'largely' health-care professionals. Dr Hinwood started his career in the 1960s as a high school teacher in Australia, England and South Africa before commencing his chiropractic studies in Canada in the mid 1970s.

With his wife Judy, he travelled extensively all over the world off the beaten track from 1969 to 1973, overland from Australia through Asia and onto Europe. They spent time in Eastern Europe and Russia during the Cold War. They drove their Landrover transAfrica and then spent many months travelling by public transport all over South America and the Caribbean before arriving in Toronto, Canada in the fall of 1973.

In late 1978, John and Judy returned to Australia and set up chiropractic practices in rural and then metropolitan communities.

In 1985, he and Judy went to Chile and found three older children, Shavela, Ignacio and Rodrigo in orphanages whom they then adopted to have an instant family.

John Hinwood is the CEO and Principal Mentor at the Centre for Powerful Practices which he founded with his wife Judy in 1991. He has an extensive client base worldwide, and publishes a weekly newsletter called Practice Pointers which is emailed to over 20,000 practitioners around the world. He has published numerous books and multi-media packages which can be purchased from the website www.powerful-practices.com, which is the ultimate resource for health-care practitioners.

He has received many awards from chiropractic organizations around the world and is the recipient of the Parker International Award and Parker Humanitarian Award for his services to the chiropractic profession worldwide. He is a Fellow of the International College of Chiropractors (FICC), the Australasian College of Chiropractors (FACC) and the Australian Institute of Management (FAIM).

In 2007 he founded Expect A Miracle Pty Ltd, a company whose sole purpose is to spread the joy of miracles around the world. In late November 2007, www.expect-a-miracle.net went online to provide a forum on the world wide web to allow people to continually post and share miracle stories 24 hours a day.

As an international speaker, he inspires his audiences into taking practical action steps to move their lives to new levels. His perspectives, humor, observations, insights into life and entertaining stories are from the heart, and they inspire and motivate people into taking positive action steps.

Print Your Own "Expect a Miracle" Cards

Expect A Miracle

On the next page you'll find three Expect a Miracle cards ready to push out of the page so you can start to hand them out to enhance your life.

An easy way to print your own cards is to go to our companion website www.expect-a-miracle.net. Go to the E-A-M Cards button at the top of the home page and just print off your own cards on your home or office printer and start handing them out.

Alternatively, you can go to your local printer and have them print your cards for you.

Using these little cards can change YOUR life and the lives of many people you come in contact with during your daily interactions in life.

"A small group of thoughtful people could change the world. Indeed, it's the only thing that ever has."

Margaret Mead

Expect A Miracle

Expect A Miracle

Expect A Miracle

Expect A Miracle

Expect A Miracle

Expect A Miracle